T0121098

THE
LIFE-GIVING
TREE

The
Revelation
of
Jesus Christ

SECOND EDITION

Pastor and Prophet Clifford Reid

WESTBOW
P R E S S®
A DIVISION OF THOMAS NELSON
& ZONDERVAN

WestBow Press books may be ordered through booksellers or by contacting:

WestBow Press
A Division of Thomas Nelson & Zondervan
1663 Liberty Drive
Bloomington, IN 47403
www.westbowpress.com
844-714-3454

Scripture taken from the King James Version of the Bible.

ISBN: 978-1-6642-3241-9 (sc)
ISBN: 978-1-6642-3240-2 (e)

Print information available on the last page.

WestBow Press rev. date: 02/24/2022

The Author's Style of Writing

The author in his writings has covered many scripture verses with an intent to establish doctrines rightly dividing the Word of Truth. This is done in his teachings so that there will be no gainsay after the topics that he deals with in *The Life-Giving Tree* are discussed. He tries to build scripture upon scripture, like precept upon precept, to fortify doctrinal truths of the Word of God. He intentionally leaves out much of human brilliance so that your faith will be established not on human excellence but on the Word of God, which liveth and abideth forever! This may appear to be a human weakness in his writings, but it really is the strength upon which the fundamental truths that he projects is established. When Jesus was tempted by the devil, he used the written Word of God to defeat him. He said, "It is written." The writer also considers that the book is largely based on happenings of the last days, figuring that the Word of God eventually will be taken away from us. He hopes that when this happens, one will strategically have a rich source of reference in the Word of God in *The Life-Giving Tree.*

I am the vine, ye are the branches, he that abideth in me, and I in him, the same bringeth forth much fruit.
—John 15:5

CONTENTS

PREFACE

The information in *The Life-Giving Tree* is revealing and quite explosive. Anyone who has gotten hold of *The Life-Giving Tree* can consider themselves privileged and fortunate. Many books have been written on some of the subjects that will be addressed herein, but none of them do so in quite a revealing, dynamic, strategic, and accurately prophetic way as this one. The writer goes beyond surface truth and gets to the depths of revelations to cause the reader to highly appreciate who Jesus is, his mission, and his divine agenda. God's plan and program is unfolding in the dynamics of biblical eschatology. The simplicity with which the truth is presented is to ensure that the most salient points are well embraced and understood, which will embolden your faith when tried and tested and will better prepare you for what is shortly ahead.

PART ONE

The Unfolding
of Jesus Christ

CHAPTER ONE

The Revelation

In Matthew 16:13, Jesus was on Mount Philippi when he asked his disciples a burning question. This question did not come about because of a lack of knowledge on his part, but it was to establish his divine sonship beyond a shadow of a doubt in the hearts of his disciples. "Whom do men say that I the son of man am?" The term *son of man* is not exclusively used to describe Jesus; there are many other Old Testament prophets who were addressed as "son of man." In Jesus's case, however, God was trying to go beyond the veil of the flesh and get to the divine essence of his being, to unfold the uniqueness of his manhood as a Son of man to which no other sons of men could attest.

In Genesis 3:15 God said that "the seed of the woman would bruise the head of the serpent and the serpent would bruise his heel." "The seed of the woman" speaks prophetically of the birth of the Son of God. First John 3:8 states, "For this purpose the son of God was manifested, that he might destroy the works of the devil."

In Luke 1:30–35, Mary encounters the angel Gabriel. The scripture reads as follows:

> And the angel said unto her, Fear not, Mary: for thou hast found favor with God. And behold, thou

shalt conceive in thy womb, and bring forth a son, and shall call his name Jesus. He shall be great and shall be called the Son of the Highest and the Lord God shall give unto him the throne of his father David. And he shall reign over the house of Jacob forever; and of his kingdom there shall be no end. Then said Mary unto the angel, How shall this be, seeing I know not a man? And the angel answered and said unto her, the Holy Ghost shall come upon thee, and the power of the Highest shall over shadow thee: therefore also that holy thing which shall be born of thee shall be called the Son of God.

Indeed the seed of the woman is Christ Jesus. The bruising or crushing of the head of the serpent deals with the deadly blow Jesus inflicted on Satan when Jesus died and gave his life as ransom for many. Hebrews 2:14–15 states, "For as much then as the children are partakers of flesh and blood, he also himself likewise took part of the same; that through death he might destroy him that had the power of death, that is, the devil. And deliver them who through fear of death were all their lifetime subject to bondage." The bruising of Jesus's heel speaks of the price he had to pay and the suffering he had to endure to bring about our salvation.

The battle was heel versus head, the heel of Jesus crushing the head of the serpent. This also shows the supremacy of Jesus over Satan. Isaiah 52:14 states, "As many were astonished at thee; his visage was so marred more than the sons of men." Isaiah 53:5 goes on to say, "But he was wounded for our transgressions, he was bruised for our iniquities: the chastisement of our peace was upon him; and with his stripes we are healed."

Jesus masterminded the devil's plans and objectives. First Corinthians 2:8 states, "For had they known it, they would not have crucified the Lord of glory."

Colossians 2:9–15 reads as follows:

For in him dwelleth all the fullness of the God head bodily. And ye are complete in him, which is the head of all principality and power. In whom also ye are circumcised with the circumcision made without hands, in putting off the body of the sins of the flesh by the circumcision of Christ. Buried with him in baptism, wherein also ye are risen with him through the faith of the operation of God, who hath raised him from the dead. And you, being dead in your sins and the uncircumcision of your flesh, hath be quickened together with him, having forgiven you all trespasses. Blotting out the hand writing of ordinances that was against us, which was contrary to us, and took it out of the way, nailing it to his cross. And having spoiled principalities and powers, he made a show of them openly, triumphing over them in it.

Praise the Lord. He went all the way to redeem us! Following are two questions Jesus asked his disciples at Caesarea Philippi: (1) "Whom do men say that I the son of man am?" (2) "But whom say ye that I am?" People today are still wrestling with these two questions. The first question is based on humankind's opinion of Jesus Christ. Humankind's opinion is not always right. In this case, the suggestions given, though noble in equating him with Jeremiah or Elias or as describing him as one of the great prophets, is not nearly close enough to declare who Jesus is. To say he was a good man is not good enough. To say he is a great prophet is not revealing enough! Remember that when John was placed in prison, he sent two of his disciples to Jesus to inquire who he was. Jesus addressed John the Baptist, two disciples, and the multitude in the manner we read about in Matthew 11:4–11, as follows:

Jesus answered and said unto them, Go and shew John again those things which ye do hear and see:

the blind receive their sight, and the lame walk, the lepers are cleansed, and the deaf hear, the dead are raised up, and the poor have the gospel preached to them. And blessed is he, whosoever shall not be offended in me. And as they departed, Jesus began to say unto the multitudes concerning John, what went ye out into the wilderness to see? A reed shaken with the wind? But what went ye out for to see? A man clothed in soft raiment? Behold, they that wear soft clothing are in kings houses. But what went ye out for to see? A prophet? Yea, I say unto you, and more than a prophet. For this is he, of whom it is written, Behold, I send my messenger before thy face, which shall prepare thy way before thee. Verily I say unto you, Among them that are born of women there hath not risen a greater than John the Baptist: notwithstanding he that is least in the kingdom of heaven is greater than he.

I will deal with the latter portion of this verse as we go along. For now, let us focus on the statement made by Jesus concerning John, namely that John was the greatest human being ever to have come forth from a woman's womb. Let's now look at John the Baptist's comments to the people about Jesus in Matthew 3:11–12: "I indeed baptize you with water unto repentance, but he that cometh after me is mightier than I, whose shoes I am not worthy to bear; he shall baptize you with the Holy Ghost, and with fire: whose fan is in his hands, and he will thoroughly purge his floor, and gather his wheat into the garner; but he will burn up the chaff with unquenchable fire." Now if Jesus declared John the Baptist as the greatest born from a woman, and if John, in his description of Jesus, said that he was not worthy to unloose Jesus's shoes, who then is Christ?

The second question was directed to Jesus's disciples. I would like to direct the same question to you: "Who do you say that I the son of man am?" Peter answered and said, "Thou art the Christ, the son of the living God." If Jesus had not provided an answer to this question, then we would have to give credit to Peter as being an extraordinarily brilliant man. But the glory goes to God. Jesus's reply to Peter was, "Blessed art thou Simon Barjona, for flesh and blood hath not revealed it unto thee, but my father which is in heaven." The revelation as to who Jesus is was not made by human ingenuity but by divine revelation. And today this statement is just as true as it was then. The Spirit of God / the Holy Ghost needs to reveal to us the true personhood of Jesus. In other words, we need to make room in our hearts to allow the Holy Spirit to unfold for us the revelation of Jesus Christ. Many times we use our human minds to understand the vastness of this majestic being called "the Son of God," but we fail miserably with our finite minds to understand his infinite nature.

The apostle Paul was such a man sold out for God. In Philippians 3:5–6 he states, "Circumcised the eight day of the stock of Israel, of the tribe of Benjamin, a Hebrew of the Hebrews; as touching the law, a Pharisee. Concerning zeal, persecuting the church; touching the righteousness which is in the law, blameless." At that time, he knew neither the plan of God nor who Jesus was. In Galatians 1:13–16 he stated, "For ye have heard of my conversation in time past in the Jewish religion, how that beyond measure I persecuted the church of God, and wasted it: And profited in the Jews' religion above many my equals in mine own nation, being more exceedingly zealous of the traditions of my fathers. But when it pleased God, who separated me from my mother's womb, and called me by his grace, to reveal his son in me, that I might preach him among the heathens; immediately I conferred not with flesh and blood."

He also stated the following in Galatians 1:8–12:

> But though we, or an angel from heaven, preach any other gospel unto you than that which we have preached unto you, let him be accursed. As we said before, so say I now again, if any man preach any other gospel unto you than that ye have received, let him be accursed. For do I now persuade men,

or God? Or do I seek to please men? For if I yet pleased men, I should not be the servant of Christ. But I certify you, brethren that the gospel which was preached of me is not after man. For I neither received it of man, neither was I taught it, but by the revelation of Jesus Christ.

SAUL'S CONVERSION

We read of this event in Acts 9:1–6, as follows:

> And Saul, yet breathing out threatenings and slaughter against the disciples of the Lord, went unto the high priest, and desired of him letters to Damascus to the synagogues, that if he found any of this way, whether they were men or women, he might bring them bound unto Jerusalem. And as he journeyed, he came near Damascus: and suddenly there shined round about him a light from heaven: And he fell to the earth, and heard a voice saying unto him, Saul, Saul, why persecutest thou me? And he said, Who art thou, Lord? And the Lord said, I am Jesus whom thou persecutest: it is hard for thee to kick against the pricks. And he trembling and astonished said, Lord, what wilt thou have me to do? And the Lord said unto him, Arise, and go into the city, and it shall be told thee what thou must do.

In Acts 26:12–16 Paul testified before King Agrippa and said the following:

> Whereupon as I went to Damascus with authority and commission from the chief priests. At midday, O king, I saw in the way a light from heaven, above the brightness of the sun, shining round about me and

them which journeyed with me. And when we were all fallen to the earth, I heard a voice speaking unto me, and saying in the Hebrew tongue, Saul, Saul, why persecutest thou me? it is hard for thee to kick against the pricks. And I said, Who art thou, Lord? And he said, I am Jesus whom thou persecute. But rise, and stand upon thy feet: for I have appeared unto thee for this purpose, to make thee a minister and a witness both of these things which thou hast seen, and of those things in the which I will appear unto thee.

Paul said the following in Philippians 3:7–14:

But what things were gain to me, those I counted loss for Christ. Yea doubtless, and I count all things but loss for the excellency of the knowledge of Christ Jesus my Lord: for whom I have suffered the loss of all things, and do count them but dung, that I may win Christ, and be found in him, not having mine own righteousness, which is of the law, but that which is through the faith of Christ, the righteousness which is of God by faith: That I may know him, and the power of his resurrection, and the fellowship of his sufferings, being made conformable unto his death; If by any means I might attain unto the resurrection of the dead. Not as though I had already attained, either were already perfect: but I follow after, if that I may apprehend that for which also I am apprehended of Christ Jesus. Brethren, I count not myself to have apprehended: but this one thing I do, forgetting those things which are behind, and reaching forth unto those things which are before, I press toward the mark for the prize of the high calling of God in Christ Jesus.

THE UNFOLDING OF JESUS CHRIST

Hebrews 1:1–3 states, "God, who at sundry times and in divers manners spake in time past unto the fathers by the prophets, hath in these last days spoken unto us by his Son, whom he hath appointed heir of all things, by whom also he made the worlds; who being the brightness of his glory, and the express image of his person, and upholding all things by the word of his power, when he had by himself purged our sins, sat down on the right hand of the Majesty on high."

Jesus Is God

First Timothy 3:16 states, "And without controversy great is the mystery of godliness: God was manifest in the flesh, justified in the Spirit, seen of angels, preached unto the Gentiles, believed on in the world, received up into glory." Our finite minds could never understand the infinite mind of God. And when we attempt to do so through human logistics, we fail miserably. But God has given to us *faith* that links humankind to God. Hebrews 11:3 states, "*Through faith we understand* that the worlds were framed by the word of God, so that things which are seen were not made of things which do appear" (emphasis added). John 1:1–3 reads, "In the beginning was the Word, and the Word was with God, and the Word was God. The same was in the beginning with God. All things were made by him; and without him was not anything made that was made." It goes on in verse 14: "And the Word was made flesh, and dwelt among us, (and we beheld his glory, the glory as of the only begotten of the Father,) full of grace and truth."

We read in John 1:10, "He was in the world, and the world was made by him, and the world knew him not."

Matthew 1:23 tells us, "Behold, a virgin shall be with child, and shall bring forth a son, and they shall call his name Emmanuel, which being interpreted is, God with us."

In John 8:56–58, Jesus said to the Jews who were questioning him, "Your father Abraham rejoiced to see my day: and he saw it, and was glad. Then said the Jews unto him, Thou art not yet fifty years old, and hast thou seen Abraham? ... Verily, verily, I say unto you, Before Abraham was, *I am*" (emphasis added). The reference is to Exodus 3:13–14: "And Moses said unto God, Behold, when I come unto the children of Israel, and shall say unto them, The God of your fathers hath sent me unto you; and they shall say to me, What is his name? What shall I say unto them? And God said unto the children of Israel, *I Am* hath sent me unto you" (emphasis added).

We read in Micah 5:2, "But thou, Bethlehem Ephratah, though thou be little among the thousands of Judah, yet out of thee shall he come forth unto me that is to be ruler in Israel; whose goings forth have been from of old, from everlasting."

Reference to the fulfilment of the above prophecies is found in Matthew 2:1–6:

> Now when Jesus was born in Bethlehem of Judaea in the days of Herod the king, behold, there came wise men from the east to Jerusalem, saying, Where is he that is born King of the Jews? for we have seen his star in the east, and are come to worship him. When Herod the king had heard these things, he was troubled, and all Jerusalem with him. And when he had gathered all the chief priests and scribes of the people together, he demanded of them where Christ should be born. And they said unto him, In Bethlehem of Judaea: for thus it is written by the prophet, and thou Bethlehem, in the land of Judah, art not the least among the princes of Judah: for out of thee shall come a Governor, that shall rule my people Israel.

We read the following in Hebrews 1:8–12:

> But unto the Son he saith, Thy throne, O God, is forever and ever: a sceptre of righteousness

is the sceptre of thy kingdom. Thou hast loved righteousness, and hated iniquity; therefore God, even thy God, hath anointed thee with the oil of gladness above *thy fellows*. And, Thou, Lord, in the beginning hast laid the foundation of the earth; and the heavens are the works of thine hands: They shall perish; but thou remainest; and they all shall wax old as doth a garment; And as a vesture shalt thou fold them up, and they shall be changed: but thou art the same, and thy years shall not fail. (emphasis added)

This scripture goes back and forward and back, showing Jesus in his pre-incarnate state, in his incarnate state when he became human, and then back into his pre-incarnate state.

WHO ARE HIS FELLOWS?

Jesus's fellows are his brethren when God became man or when God chose to be born of a virgin. A new breed was made possible, a race called "sons of God," Jesus being the first among many brethren. You and I are saved by his grace! Psalm 22:22 reads, "I will declare thy name unto my brethren: in the midst of the congregation will I praise thee." Romans 8:29 reads, "For whom he did foreknow, he also did predestinate to be conformed to the image of his Son, that he might be the firstborn among many brethren." We read in 1 Corinthians 15:47–49, "The first man is of the earth, earthy: *the second man is the Lord from heaven. As is the earthy, such are they also that are earthy: and as is the heavenly, such are they also that are heavenly. And as we have borne the image of the earthy, we shall also bear the image of the heavenly*" (emphasis added).

We read in 1 John 1:1–2, "That which was from the beginning, which we have heard, which we have seen with our eyes, which we have looked upon, and our hands have handled, of the Word of life; (For the life was manifested, and we have seen it, and bear witness, and shew unto you that eternal life, which was with the Father, and was manifested unto us)."

First John 5:19–21 reads, "And we know that we are of God, and the whole world lieth in wickedness. And we know that the Son of God is come, and hath given us an understanding, that we may know him that is true, and we are in him that is true, even in his Son Jesus Christ. This is the true God, and eternal life. Little children, keep yourselves from idols. Amen." All things created, all things that are in heaven and on earth, visible and invisible, whether they be thrones, or dominions, or principalities, or powers—all things were created by him and for him (Colossians 1:16) And he is before all things, and by him all things consist. He is the head of the body, the church, who is the beginning, the firstborn from the dead, so that in all things he might have preeminence.

We read the following in Philippians 2:5–11:

> Let this mind be in you, which was also in Christ Jesus: Who, being in the form of God, thought it not robbery to be equal with God: But made himself of no reputation, and took upon him the form of a servant, and was made in the likeness of men: And being found in fashion as a man, he humbled himself, and became obedient unto death, even the death of the cross. Wherefore God also hath highly exalted him, and given him a name which is above every name: That at the name of Jesus every knee should bow, of things in heaven, and things in earth, and things under the earth; And that every tongue should confess that Jesus Christ is Lord, to the glory of God the Father.

Isaiah 9:6–7 reads, "For unto us a child is born, unto us a son is given: and the government shall be upon his shoulder: and his name shall be called Wonderful, Counsellor, the mighty God, the everlasting Father, the Prince of Peace. Of the increase of his government and peace there shall be no end, upon the throne of

David, and upon his kingdom, to order it, and to establish it with judgment and with justice from henceforth even for ever. The zeal of the Lord of hosts will perform this."

Psalm 2:7–8 tells us, "I will declare the decree: the Lord hath said unto me, Thou art my Son; this day have I begotten thee. Ask of me, and I shall give thee the heathen for thine inheritance, and the uttermost parts of the earth for thy possession."

We read in John 3:16, "For God so loved the world, that he gave his only begotten Son, that whosoever believeth in him should not perish, but have everlasting life." When was the son of God begotten? About two thousand years ago! Do not believe that the begotten Son of God was begotten millions or even billions of years ago. *He was begotten* when he was made *flesh*. In other words, if humankind had not sinned and there was no need of redemption, no need for Jesus to shed his blood for our sins, then we would never have heard about the being called "Son of God." It was only for the sake of redemption that God robed himself in flesh to pay the price that he did not owe (i.e., death) to ransom us from sin. Do you understand this statement? *God never had an eternal son, but Jesus is God's eternal son by reason of his inheritance!* Where did he come from? Had humankind not sinned, Jesus still would have existed as God, the very God. Let us not try to make Jesus a creation of God. He is responsible for the creation of everything.

Genesis 1:1 says, "In the beginning God created the heaven and the earth." Jesus Christ is immutable. "Jesus Christ the same yesterday, and today, and for ever." We read in Hebrews 13:8, "The heavens are the works of thy hands; they shall perish; but thou remainst; and they all shall wax old as doth a garment; and as a vesture shalt thou fold them up, and they shall be changed but thou art the same and thy years shall not fail."

CHRIST IS OMNIPOTENT

Matthew 28:18 reads, "All power is given unto me in heaven and in earth." We find in John 1:3, 10, "All things were made by him; ...

and without him was not anything was made by him, and the world knew him not."

CHRIST IS OMNISCIENT

Matthew 9:4 reads, "And Jesus knowing their thoughts said, Wherefore think ye evil in your hearts?"

We read in John 2:24-25, "But Jesus did not commit himself unto them, because he knew all men, and needed not that any should testify of man: for he knew what was in man."

John 6:64 reads, "But there are some of you that believe not. For Jesus knew from the beginning who they were that believed not, and who should betray him."

We find in Colossians 2:3, "In whom are hid all the treasures of wisdom and knowledge."

CHRIST IS OMNIPRESENT

Matthew 18:20 reads, "For where two or three are gathered together in my name, there am I in the midst of them."

We find in Matthew 28:20, "Teaching them to observe all things whatsoever I have commanded you: and, lo, I am with you always, even unto the end of the world. Amen."

SCRIPTURE SUPPORTING JESUS AS THE SON OF GOD

- Mark 1:1: "The beginning of the gospel of Jesus Christ, the Son of God." John 10:36, "Say ye of him, whom the Father hath sanctified, and sent into the world, Thou blasphemest; because I said, I am the Son of God?"
- John 11:4: "When Jesus heard that, he said, This sickness is not unto death, but for the glory of God, that the Son of God might be glorified thereby."

- Acts 8:37: "And Philip said, If thou believest with all thine heart, thou mayest. And he answered and said, I believe that Jesus Christ is the Son of God."
- Acts 9:20: "And straightway he preached Christ in the synagogues, that he is the Son of God."
- 2 Corinthians 1:19: "For the Son of God, Jesus Christ, who was preached among you by us, even by me and Silvanus and Timothy, was not yea and nay, but in him was yea."
- Galatians 2:20: "I am crucified with Christ: nevertheless I live; yet not I, but Christ liveth in me: and the life which I now live in the flesh I live by the faith of the Son of God, who loved me, and gave himself for me."
- Ephesians 4:13: "Till we all come in the unity of the faith, and of the knowledge of the Son of God, unto a perfect man, unto the measure of the stature of the fulness of Christ."
- Hebrews 4:14: "Seeing then that we have a great high priest, that is passed into the heavens, Jesus the Son of God, let us hold fast our profession."
- 1 John 4:15: "Whosoever shall confess that Jesus is the Son of God, God dwelleth in him, and he in God."
- 1 John 5:10–11: "He that believeth on the Son of God hath the witness in himself: he that believeth not God hath made him a liar; because he believeth not the record that God gave of his Son. And this is the record that God hath given to us eternal life, and this life is in his Son."
- 1 John 5:20: "And we know that the Son of God is come, and hath given us an understanding, that we may know him that is true, and we are in him that is true, even in his Son Jesus Christ. This is the true God, and eternal life."
- Revelation 2:18: "And unto the angel of the church in Thyatira write; These things saith the Son of God, who hath his eyes like unto a flame of fire, and his feet are like fine brass."

CHAPTER TWO

The Significance of His Sonship in Relation to the Redeemed

The apostle Paul in Ephesians 1:17–23 states as follows:

> That the God of our Lord Jesus Christ, the Father of glory, may give unto you the spirit of wisdom and revelation in the knowledge of him. The eyes of your understanding being enlightened; that ye may know what is the hope of his calling, and what the riches of the glory of his inheritance in the saints. And what is the exceeding greatness of his power to us-ward who believe, according to the working of his mighty power. Which he wrought in Christ, when he raised him from the dead, and set him at his own right hand in the heavenly places. Far above all principality, and power, and might, and dominion, and every name that is named, not only in this world, but also in that which is to come: And hath put all things under his feet, and gave him to be the head over all things to the church. Which is his body, the fulness of him that filleth all in all.

God's glorious plan for redemption is to make us sons and daughters of God by using Jesus as the progenitor of a new race of beings called sons of God. Just as Adam was the progenitor of the human race, so Jesus is the progenitor of a new species of being called sons of God. Alleluia! Praise the Lord. John 1:11–12 states, "He came unto his own, and his own received him not. But as many as received him, to them gave he power to become the sons of God, even to them that believe on his name."

First Corinthians 15:47–49 states, "The first man is of the earth, earthy: the second man is the Lord from heaven. As is the earthy, such are they also that are earthy: and as is the heavenly, such are they also that are heavenly. And as we have borne the image of the earthy, we shall also bear the image of the heavenly." Wow! God will make sons and daughters of God of all those who would repent of their sins, rely on the finished work of the grace of God in Christ Jesus, and accept him as Lord and Savior of their lives. Those who call upon thee name of the Lord shall be saved. Those who open their hearts and ask Jesus to come in shall be saved. Those who ask Jesus to wash away their sins in his own blood and give them his Holy Spirit shall be saved. Psalm 22 deals prophetically with the scenes of the cross and the things that Christ Jesus accomplished as a result of his death, burial, and resurrection.

Psalm 22:22 states, "I will declare thy name unto my brethren: in the midst of the congregation will I praise thee." Through the work of grace, Jesus calls us his brethren. Ephesians 5:30 states, "For we are members of his body, of his flesh, and of his bones." We must remember that this can only come about by the work of grace. Ephesians 2:13–22 reads as follows:

> But now in Christ Jesus ye who sometimes were far off are made nigh by the blood of Christ. For he is our peace, who hath made both one, and hath broken down the middle wall of partition between us. Having abolished in his flesh the enmity, even the law of commandments contained in ordinances;

for to make in himself of twain one new man, so making peace. And that he might reconcile both unto God in one body by the cross, having slain the enmity thereby. And came and preached peace to you which were afar off, and to them that were nigh. For through him we both have access by one Spirit unto the Father. Now therefore ye are no more strangers and foreigners, but fellow citizens with the saints, and of the household of God. And are built upon the foundation of the apostles and prophets, Jesus Christ himself being the chief corner stone. In whom all the building fitly framed together groweth unto an holy temple in the Lord. In whom ye also are builded together for a habitation of God through the Spirit.

Romans 8:15–29 states the following:

For ye have not received the spirit of bondage again to fear; but ye have received the Spirit of adoption, whereby we cry, Abba, Father. The Spirit itself beareth witness with our spirit, that we are the children of God: And if children, then heirs; heirs of God, and joint-heirs with Christ; if so be that we suffer with him, that we may be also glorified together. For I reckon that the sufferings of this present time are not worthy to be compared with the glory which shall be revealed in us. For the earnest expectation of the creature waiteth for the manifestation of the sons of God. For the creature was made subject to vanity, not willingly, but by reason of him who hath subjected the same in hope, because the creature itself also shall be delivered from the bondage of corruption into the glorious liberty of the children of God. For we know that the whole creation groaneth and travaileth in pain together until now. And not only they, but ourselves also, which have the firstfruits of the Spirit, even we ourselves groan within ourselves, waiting for the adoption, to wit, the redemption of our body. For we are saved by hope: but hope that is seen is not hope: for what a man seeth, why doth he yet hope for? But if we hope for that we see not, then do we with patience wait for it. Likewise the Spirit also helpeth our infirmities: for we know not what we should pray for as we ought: but the Spirit itself maketh intercession for us with groanings which cannot be uttered. And he that searcheth the hearts knoweth what is the mind of the Spirit, because he maketh intercession for the saints according to the will of God. And we know that all things work together for good to them that love God, to them who are the called according to his purpose. For whom he did foreknow, he also did predestinate to be conformed to the image of his Son, *that he might be the firstborn among many brethren.* (emphasis added)

Wow! Jesus is the firstborn among many brethren. Who are the many brethren? You and I who have accepted him. We are part of the new race of people called "sons of God."

First John 3:1–3 states, "Behold, what manner of love the Father hath bestowed upon us, that we should be called the sons of God: therefore the world knoweth us not, because it knew him not. Beloved, now are we the sons of God, and it doth not yet appear what we shall be: but we know that, when he shall appear, *we shall be like him*; for we shall see him as he is. And every man that hath this hope in him purifieth himself, even as he is pure" (emphasis added).

Second Corinthians 5:17 states, "Therefore if any man be in Christ, *he is a new creature*: old things are passed away; behold, all things are become new" (emphasis added). We who have accepted Jesus are *new creations called sons of God, Jesus being the firstborn among many brethren.* I must keep repeating this vivid truth until it gets into your spirit.

Matthew 13:43 states, "Then shall the *righteous shine forth as the sun* in the kingdom of their Father. *Who hath ears* to hear, let him hear" (emphasis added). *We shall share in his glory throughout the countless ages of eternity.*

First Peter 5:10 states, "But the God of all grace, *who hath called us unto his eternal glory by Christ Jesus,* after that ye have suffered a while, make you perfect, stablish, strengthen, settle you" (emphasis added). You can now see clearly that it is only through Jesus Christ that you can be a partaker of this blessing.

Second Peter 1:3–4 states, "According as his divine power hath given unto us all things that pertain unto life and godliness, through the knowledge of *him that hath called us to glory and virtue.* Whereby are given unto us exceeding great and precious promises: that by these ye might *be partakers of the divine nature,* having escaped the corruption that is in the world through lust" (emphasis added).

GLORY AFTER SUFFERING

Second Corinthians 4:17 states, "For our light affliction, which is but for a moment, worketh for us a far more exceeding and *eternal weight of glory*" (emphasis added). In Romans 8:18, Saint Paul states, "For I reckon that the sufferings of this present time are not worthy to be compared with the *glory which shall be revealed in us*" (emphasis added).

First Corinthians 15:40–49 reads as follows:

> There are also celestial bodies, and bodies terrestrial:
> but the glory of the celestial is one, and the glory of
> the terrestrial is another. There is one glory of the
> sun, and another glory of the moon, and another
> glory of the stars: for one star differeth from another

star in glory. So also is the resurrection of the dead. It is sown in corruption; it is raised in incorruption. It is sown in dishonour; *it is raised in glory*; it is sown in weakness; it is raised in power. It is sown a natural body; it is raised a spiritual body. There is a natural body, and there is a spiritual body. And so it is written, The first man Adam was made a living soul; the last Adam was made a quickening spirit. Howbeit that was not first which is spiritual, but that which is natural; and afterward that which is spiritual. The first man is of the earth, earthy: the second man is the Lord *from heaven*. As is the earthy, such are they also that are earthy: and as is the heavenly, such are they also that are heavenly. *And as we have borne the image of the earthy, we shall also bear the image of the heavenly.* (emphasis added)

Matthew 13:43 states, "Then shall the righteous shine forth as the *sun* in the kingdom of their Father. Who hath *ears to hear*, let him hear" (emphasis added).

Daniel 12:2–3 speaks of the resurrection of the righteous dead and also of the resurrection of the wicked dead. It reads as follows: "And many of them that sleep in the dust of the earth shall awake, some to everlasting life, and some to shame and everlasting contempt. *And they that be wise shall shine as the brightness of the firmament*; and they that turn many to righteousness as the *stars for ever and ever*" (emphasis added). In Revelation 18:1, an angel came down from heaven, and his glory was so bright that it lit up the earth. We read thus: "And after these things I saw another angel come down from heaven, having great power; and the earth was lightened with his glory."

The church of Jesus Christ is called to share in the glory of God. Romans 5:1–2 states, "Therefore being justified by faith, we have peace with God through our Lord Jesus Christ. *By whom also we have access by faith into this grace wherein we stand, and rejoice in hope of the glory of God"* (emphasis added).

Second Corinthians 3:17–18 states, "Now the Lord is that Spirit: and where the Spirit of the Lord is, there is liberty. *But we all, with open face beholding as in a glass the glory of the Lord, are changed into the same image from glory to glory, even as by the Spirit of the Lord"* (emphasis added).

First Thessalonians 2:12 states, "That ye would walk worthy of God, who hath *called you unto his kingdom and glory"* (emphasis added).

Second Thessalonians 1:4–5 states, "So that we ourselves glory in you in the churches of God for your patience and faith in all your persecutions and tribulations that ye endure: Which is a manifest token of the righteous judgment of God, that ye may be counted worthy of the kingdom of God, for which ye also suffer."

First Peter 5:10 states, *"But the God of all grace, who hath called us unto his eternal glory by Christ Jesus,* after that ye have suffered a while, make you perfect, stablish, strengthen, settle you" (emphasis added).

Second Peter 1:3–4 states, "According as his divine power hath given unto us all things that pertain unto life and godliness, through the knowledge of him that hath called us to glory and virtue. Whereby are given unto us exceeding great and precious promises: that by these ye might be partakers of the *divine nature,* having escaped the corruption that is in the world through lust" (emphasis added). As sons of God, *we are now members of the body of Christ and will share in his eternal glory forever and ever.*

Can you imagine the glory we shall share with our blessed Redeemer? Scientists tell us that light travels at the speed of 186,000 miles per second and that it takes hundreds of light-years before we are able to see on earth the light that comes from some of these stars. They are very far away! But this just scratches the surface as many stars are so far away that we cannot even see them. Yet in Acts 9, when Saul/Paul saw the glory of Jesus in a moment of shining from beyond the farthest star, even in his excellent glory he was blinded by that light. Wow! That's the type of glory we will be sharing with Jesus! Please give your life to Jesus. Don't miss God's great plan of salvation that he has provided for us through Jesus Christ. Forsake your sin. It doesn't matter how painful the cost may be, just give your life to Jesus. Paul said in Romans 10:9-13, "That if thou shalt *confess with thy mouth* the Lord Jesus, and shalt *believe in thine heart* that God hath raised him from the dead, thou shalt be saved. For with the heart man believeth unto righteousness; and with the mouth confession is made unto salvation. For the scripture saith, Whosoever believeth on him shall not be ashamed. For there is no difference between the Jew and the Greek: for the same Lord over all is rich unto all that call upon him. For whosoever shall call upon the name of the Lord shall be saved" (emphasis added).

I would like to look into the book of Revelation, the last book of the New Testament, and do a practical study of it. I assure you that the truths will be quite revealing. God is opening up the book of Revelation to his saints as the time is at hand. As the drama of the last days unfolds itself, prophetic revelations must be clearly understood by God's people that will help empower them and prepare them for the challenges ahead. To be forewarned is to be forearmed.

Daniel 12:10 states, "Many shall be purified, and made white, *and tried*; but the wicked shall do wickedly: and none of the wicked shall understand; but the wise shall understand" (emphasis added). Also, many shall fall away. I pray that you and I will not be a part of that large group but that we will fall in love with Jesus and develop an intimacy with him that will preserve us unto the day of the redemption of our bodies.

Second Thessalonians 2:3 states, "Let no man deceive you by any means: for that day shall not come, except there come a falling away first, and that man of sin be revealed, the son of perdition." In other words, before the rapturing of the saints to glory, (a) there will be a falling away and (b) the Antichrist will be revealed.

We will deal with these issues as we get into the book of Revelation.

I do not purpose to know everything that must be known. I believe that as the body of Christ, we, God's many saints, will be given different degrees of revelation so we may build upon the truths that are revealed—this so that no person gets the glory. The glory belongs to God and God alone.

Nevertheless, I can assure the reader that quite a bit of information will be discussed that has never been explained before. We will not look into every detail but will cover major topics.

PART TWO

The Book
of Revelation

CHAPTER THREE

A Close Reading of Revelation

REVELATION CHAPTER 1

All disputes concerning who Jesus Christ really is can be solved by taking a deep look at how God presented Jesus Christ. The book of Revelation is not a revelation of how Jesus presents himself, nor is it a revelation of how the apostles saw Jesus, but it is an unfolding of the personhood and divine character of Jesus by God the Father. Therefore, I urge you to put away human and religious biases and accept God's presentation of Jesus. Revelation 1:1 states, "The Revelation of Jesus Christ, *which God gave unto him*, to shew unto his servants things which must shortly come to pass; and he sent and signified it by his angel unto his servant John" (emphasis added). Verse 3 states that there's a blessing to those who read and hear the words of the prophecy, and the blessings are ensured by those who keep to those things that are written in the book of Revelation. The reader is blessed by the things he or she hears, by the things he or she reads. Do you embrace the promises laid out in Revelation? Do you claim them as yours? Are you willing to make the sacrifice, to pay the price, and to do whatever lies within your power so that you may be a recipient of all the blessed promises in this book? Nothing should hold you back from doing so.

Verse 4 reads, "John to the seven churches which are in Asia: Grace be unto you, and peace, from him which is, and which was, and which is to come; and from the seven Spirits which are before his throne." We know that the number 7 is God's number of completeness and perfection, so the message is also for all the churches at large. It also makes reference to the seven church ages down through the centuries. The seven spirits that are before God's throne are the seven manifestations of the Spirit of God. For example, Isaiah 11:1–3 states, "And there shall come forth a rod out of the stem of Jesse, and a Branch shall grow out of his roots: And the spirit of the Lord shall rest upon him, (1) the spirit of wisdom and (2) understanding, (3) the spirit of counsel (4) and might, (5) the spirit of knowledge (6) and of the fear of the Lord; (7) and shall make him of quick understanding in the fear of the Lord: and he shall not judge after the sight of his eyes, neither reprove after the hearing of his ears." As I have said, we are not looking at every detail in the book of Revelation, but we will be highlighting the aspects that deal with the revelation of Jesus and some pertinent related factors that enrich the subject matter.

Verses 5 and 6 depict Jesus as the following things:

- the faithful witness
- the first begotten of the dead
- the Prince of the kings of the earth
- the One who loves us
- the One who washes us of our sins in his own blood
- the One who has made us kings and priests unto God his Father.

To him be the glory and dominion forever and ever. Amen.

Verse 7 reads, "Behold, he cometh with clouds; and every eye shall see him, and they also which pierced him: and all kindreds of the earth shall wail because of him. Even so, amen."

"When Jesus was tried before the high priest, he held his peace against his accusers. But the high priest said unto him, I adjure thee by the living God, that thou tell us whether thou be the Christ the

Son of God. *Jesus said unto him, Thou hast said, nevertheless I say unto you, here after shall ye see the Son of man sitting on the right hand of power and coming in the clouds of heaven.* Then the high priest rent his clothes, saying He hath spoken blasphemy" (Matthew 26:63–65, emphasis added). A high priest's garment must never be torn under any circumstances. Therefore, what the high priest did unwittingly was to have ceremoniously put an end to the old order of priesthood so a new order of priesthood could come forth. Jesus came after the Order of Melchizedek, with no beginning of days and no ending of years. "Jesus ever liveth to make intercession for us." Hebrews 5:10 reads, "Called of God an high priest after the order of Melchizedek."

Now let's look back to verse 7: "Behold, he cometh with clouds; and every eye shall see him, and they also which pierced him: and all kindreds of the earth shall wail because of him. Even so, amen."

When will this event take place? Is it at the rapture of the church, or is it at his Second Coming? Certainly it is not at the rapture (catching away of the saints). The rapture will take place before his Second Coming. It will take place so fast that mortal eyes will not be able to behold this great event.

First Corinthians 15:51–57 describes the rapture:

> Behold, I shew you a mystery; We shall not all sleep, but we shall all be changed. *In a moment, in the twinkling of an eye,* at the last trump: for the trumpet shall sound, and the dead shall be raised incorruptible, and we shall be changed. For this corruptible must put on incorruption, and this mortal must put on immortality. So when this corruptible shall have put on incorruption, and this mortal shall have put on immortality, then shall be brought to pass the saying that is written, Death is swallowed up in victory. O death, where is thy sting? O grave, where is thy victory? The sting of death is sin; and the strength of sin is the law. But thanks

be to God, which giveth us the victory through our Lord Jesus Christ. (emphasis added)

Generally, whenever Jesus speaks of his Second Coming, he is speaking of returning to the battle of Armageddon to set up his kingdom on earth for one thousand years. We need to know the difference between the rapture and his Second Coming, with the clouds of heaven, to set up his kingdom on earth. The rapture is when he returns *for* his church.

First Thessalonians 4:15–18 reads as follows:

> For this we say unto you by the word of the Lord, that we which are alive and remain unto the coming of the Lord shall not prevent them which are asleep. For the Lord himself shall descend from heaven with a shout, with the voice of the archangel, and with the trump of God: and the dead in Christ shall rise first: Then we which are alive and remain shall be caught up together with them in the clouds, to meet the Lord in the air: and so shall we ever be with the Lord. Wherefore comfort one another with these words.

The rapture will take place a few years before his Second Coming.

Revelation 19:7–8 states, "Let us be glad and rejoice, and give honour to him: for the marriage of the Lamb is come, and his wife hath made herself ready. And to her was granted that she should be arrayed in fine linen, clean and white: for the fine linen is the righteousness of saints."

In Revelation 19:11–14 we read, "And I saw heaven opened, and behold a white horse; and he that sat upon him was called Faithful and True, and in righteousness he doth judge and make war. His eyes were as a flame of fire, and on his head were many crowns; and he had a name written, that no man knew, but he himself. And he was clothed with a vesture dipped in blood: and his name is called the

Word of God. And the armies which were in heaven followed him upon white horses, *clothed in fine linen, white and clean*" (emphasis added).

This army is the bride of Christ. Marriage in deed has been consummated in verse 7; the bride is now called the *wife* of the Lamb, Jesus Christ. She has gone through the bema judgment, and her clothing is now to its finest elegance. After the church is raptured, she will have to go through the bema judgment for rewards. The bema judgment is geared not for condemnation but for purification and rewards. While the judgments of God's wrath are poured out on earth, the bema judgment will be taking place in heaven. When it is completed, one may say, "*Alas! Alas!*"

We read in Revelation 19:7, "Let us be glad and rejoice, and give honour to him: for the marriage of the Lamb is come, and his *wife* hath made herself ready" (emphasis added).

Romans 14:10 states, "But why dost thou judge thy brother? or why dost thou set at nought thy brother? for we shall all stand before the *judgment seat* of Christ" (which is the bema judgment; emphasis added).

TO GET YOUR REWARD

We read in 1 Corinthians 3:13–15 about getting our reward: "Every man's work shall be made manifest: for the day shall declare it, because it shall be revealed by fire; and the fire shall try every man's work of what sort it is. If any man's work abide which he hath built thereupon, he shall receive a reward. If any man's work shall be burned, he shall suffer loss: but he himself shall be saved; yet so as by fire."

So you can clearly see the bride of Christ before she goes through the bema judgment clothed with white robes. But as she prepares for the wedding ceremony, she is allowed or is granted the favor of passing through the bema judgment, where she comes out with her clothing to its highest elegance, prepared for the wedding (see Revelation 7 and 8). I repeat, at the rapture, Jesus comes *for* his bride, whereas at his Second Coming, he comes *with* his bride (wife).

Let's look at another scripture where Jesus prophesied of his Second Coming, Matthew 24:26–28: "Wherefore if they shall say unto you, Behold, he is in the desert; go not forth: behold, he is in the secret chambers; believe it not. For as the lightning cometh out of the east, and shineth even unto the west; so shall also the coming of the Son of man be. For wheresoever the carcase is, there will the eagles be gathered together."

So you can see that (1) his coming will be seen by all just as the lighting shines from the east to the west. This coincides with Revelation 1:7, which says all eyes shall see him. (2) At his Second Coming, he will give another sign: "Where so ever the carcass is there will the eagles be gathered together." In other words, at his Second Coming the armies of the nations of the world that come up against him will be slaughtered, and the soldiers' dead bodies will be given as food for the eagles that have gone through a period of starvation by reason of the harsh judgments that will have been taking place during that period.

Revelation 19:17–18, 21 reads as follows:

> And I saw an angel standing in the sun; and he cried with a loud voice, saying to all the fowls that fly in the midst of heaven, Come and gather yourselves together unto the supper of the great God; that ye may eat the flesh of kings, and the flesh of captains, and the flesh of mighty men, and the flesh of horses, and of them that sit on them, and the flesh of all men, both free and bond, both small and great. ... And the *remnant were slain with the sword of him that sat upon the horse, which sword proceeded out of his mouth: and all the fowls were filled with their flesh.* (emphasis added)

Does this scripture remind you of the prophecy Jesus gave in Matthew 24:28? Yes, it is very accurate!

His Second Coming will be so dramatic that they who pierced

him in his side and through his hands and feet shall behold the glorious spectacle. These men are still alive in Sheol, waiting for the resurrection of the ungodly dead (Revelation 20:11–15). The various tribes of the earth will wail at Jesus's coming. Even so, come, Lord Jesus. Humankind will then have to come to terms with the fact that the God of the Bible, the God of Abraham, Isaac, and Jacob, is the only true and living God. Every knee shall bow and every tongue shall confess that Jesus Christ is Lord, to the glory of God the Father.

Revelation 1:8 reads, "I am Alpha and Omega, the beginning and the ending, saith the Lord, which is, and which was, and which is to come, the Almighty."

This statement puts God's signature on the revelation that is unfolding. He shall bring it to pass.

We read in verses 10–11, "I was in the Spirit on the Lord's day, and heard behind me a great voice, as of a trumpet. Saying, I am Alpha and Omega, the first and the last: and, What thou seest, write in a book, and send it unto the seven churches which are in Asia; unto Ephesus, and unto Smyrna, and unto Pergamos, and unto Thyatira, and unto Sardis, and unto Philadelphia, and unto Laodicea." Note that the same description given of God is the same description given for Jesus the Son of man.

Verses 12–13 read, "And I turned to see the voice that spake with me. And being turned, I saw seven golden candlesticks. And in the midst of the seven candlesticks one like unto the Son of man, clothed with a garment down to the foot, and girt about the paps with a golden girdle." This Son of man is none other than Jesus Christ. Let's look briefly at Isaiah 44:6: "Thus saith the Lord the King of Israel, and his redeemer the Lord of hosts; I am the first, and I am the last; and beside me there is no God."

God the Father is revealing Jesus as the First and the Last, as God, the very God besides whom there is no God. This is indeed a great mystery. I would suggest that you just believe it. It is true! First John 5:20 states, "And we know that the Son of God is come, and hath given us an understanding, that we may know him that is true, and we are in him that is true, even in his Son Jesus Christ. *This is the true*

God, and eternal life" (emphasis added). First Timothy 3:16 states, "And without controversy great is the mystery of godliness: God was manifest in the flesh, justified in the Spirit, seen of angels, preached unto the Gentiles, believed on in the world, received up into glory."

God, in Isaiah 44:6, calls himself (a) King of Israel, (b) Redeemer, (c) the Lord of hosts, (d) the First, and (e) the Last. All these titles are intrinsic descriptions of the nature of Jesus Christ. However, the title "Lord of hosts" may be challenged. Let's briefly look at Psalm 24:7–10, with Psalm 24 being a messianic psalm. As the Holy Spirit moves upon King David to proclaim the completed work of the cross, David says, "Lift up your heads, O ye gates; and be ye lift up, ye everlasting doors; and the King of glory shall come in. Who is this King of glory? The Lord strong and mighty, the Lord mighty in battle. Lift up your heads, O ye gates; even lift them up, ye everlasting doors; and the King of glory shall come in. Who is this King of glory? *The Lord of hosts*, he is the King of glory" (emphasis added).

Indeed, *Jesus is the King of glory the Lord of hosts*. As Jesus ascended into heaven, the angels sang this welcoming song: "Having spoiled principalities and powers, he made a show of them openly triumphing over them in it" (Colossians 2:15). Jesus is the mighty conqueror.

When John saw the resurrected Christ, he said the following:

> His head and his hair were white like wool, as white as snow; and his eyes were as a flame of fire. And his feet like into fine brass, as if they burned in a furnace; and his voice as the sound of many waters. And he had in his right hand seven stars: and out of his mouth went a sharp two-edged sword: and his countenance was as the sun shineth in his strength. And when I saw him, I fell at his feet as dead. And he laid his right hand upon me, saying unto me, *Fear not; I am the first and the last: I am he that liveth, and was dead; and, behold, I am alive for evermore, amen; and have the keys of hell and of death.* (Revelation 1:14–18, emphasis added)

Ephesians 4:8–10 states, "Wherefore he saith, When he ascended up on high, he led captivity captive, and gave gifts unto men. Now that he ascended, what is it but that he also descended first into the lower parts of the earth? He that descended is the same also that ascended up far above all heavens, that he might fill all things."

Acts 1:9 reads, "And when he had spoken these things, while they beheld, he was taken up; and a cloud received him out of their sight."

Jesus has conquered Satan through his death, burial, and resurrection. Hebrews 2:14 states, "Forasmuch then as the children are partakers of flesh and blood, he also himself likewise took part of the same; that through death he might destroy him that had the power of death, that is, the devil."

Praise the Lord! Our Savior Jesus has the keys of hell and of death. He is alive and lives forevermore. Amen!

Matthew 28:5–6 reads, "And the angel answered and said unto the women, Fear not ye: for I know that ye seek Jesus, which was crucified. He is not here: for he is risen, as he said. Come, see the place where the Lord lay." Jesus is now seated at the right hand of God the Father, making intercession on our behalf. What a Savior!

REVELATION CHAPTERS 2–3

These chapters deal with the messages that the Lord Jesus Christ gives to the seven churches. Much work has been done by Bible scholars to identify the significance of the seven churches and the prophetic time of the period of their beginning and ending. The last church age refers to the Laodicean church, which began in 1900 and continues to date. So I will now move on to chapter 4 of Revelation.

REVELATION CHAPTER 4

We read in verses 1–2, "After this I looked, and, behold, a door was opened in heaven: and the first voice which I heard was as it were of a trumpet talking with me; which said, Come up hither, and I will shew thee things which must be hereafter. And immediately I was in the spirit: and, behold, a throne was set in heaven, and one sat on the throne."

These two verses are so simple that the smallest child could understand them, yet some theologians take this scripture and make it very complicated, saying it means things that it was never intended to mean. A door was opened in heaven and John was invited to come up for the sole purpose of showing him the things that must be hereafter.

God says what he means and God means what he says. This scripture has nothing to do with the rapture of the church and must not be taken to mean that. Such a concept is quite misleading to the body of Christ. Whenever the rapture of the church is mentioned, it is clearly stated; there is no ambiguity. Since the time I was a child, I have heard of theologians referring to this event as the rapture of the church. I have never swallowed that pill and never will.

First Thessalonians 4:15–18 reads as follows:

> For this we say unto you by the word of the Lord, that we which are alive and remain unto the coming of the Lord shall not prevent them which are asleep. For the Lord himself shall descend from heaven with a shout, with the voice of the archangel, and with the trump of God: and the dead in Christ shall rise first: Then we which are alive and remain shall be caught up together with them in the clouds, to meet the Lord in the air: and so shall we ever be with the Lord. Wherefore comfort one another with these words.

First Corinthians 15:51–58 reads as follows:

> Behold, I shew you a mystery; We shall not all sleep, but we shall all be changed, in a moment, in the twinkling of an eye, at the last trump: for

the trumpet shall sound, and the dead shall be
raised incorruptible, and we shall be changed. For
this corruptible must put on incorruption, and
this mortal must put on immortality. So when this
corruptible shall have put on incorruption, and this
mortal shall have put on immortality, then shall be
brought to pass the saying that is written, Death is
swallowed up in victory. O death, where is thy sting?
O grave, where is thy victory? The sting of death is
sin; and the strength of sin is the law. But thanks
be to God, which giveth us the victory through our
Lord Jesus Christ. Therefore, my beloved brethren,
be ye steadfast, unmovable, always abounding in the
work of the Lord, forasmuch as ye know that your
labor is not in vain in the Lord.

Revelation 4:2 reads, "And immediately I was in the spirit: and,
behold, a throne was set in heaven, and one sat on the throne."
When the rapture takes place, not only our spirits but also our
bodies will be raised from the grave and transformed. Contrast this
experience with what is described in 2 Corinthians 12:1–5. Here
Paul's experience was very real and dramatic; he had many visions
and revelations of Jesus, but in this instance he was unable to tell
whether this experience of being caught up was while he was within
his body or whether he was out of his body (spirit only). We read the
following in 2 Corinthians 12:1–5:

It is not expedient for me doubtless to glory. I will
come to visions and revelations of the Lord. I knew a
man in Christ above fourteen years ago, (whether in
the body, I cannot tell; or whether out of the body, I
cannot tell: God knoweth;) such an one caught up to
the third heaven. And I knew such a man, (whether
in the body, or out of the body, I cannot tell: God
knoweth;) how that he was caught up into paradise,

and heard unspeakable words, which it is not lawful for a man to utter. Of such an one will I glory: yet of myself I will not glory, but in mine infirmities.

Remember reading Matthew 27:51–53, which states, "And, behold, the veil of the temple was rent in twain from the top to the bottom; and the earth did quake, and the rocks rent; and the graves were opened; and many bodies of the saints which slept arose, and came out of the graves after his resurrection, and went into the holy city, and appeared unto many." This group of saints is called "Christ's first fruits" (1 Corinthians 15:20). What the church of Christ is looking forward to is the rapture—"they that are Christ at his coming" (1 Corinthians 15:23–24). For extensive teachings on this subject matter, you may refer to my book *Standing on the Edge of Eternity*.

Let's continue.

"And behold, a throne was set in heaven and one sat on the throne." We must remember that from here on, John was seeing things that were futuristic. This quotation must not therefore be taken to mean that John entered heaven and, as a silent observer, began to see what heaven was like and the events that took place. For example, in Revelation 8:1 there was silence in heaven for half an hour. Was there really silence in heaven for half an hour at the time John received the vision? Certainly not. But when the seventh seal is broken in the near future, there will be silence in heaven at the time of its breaking. That explains why a throne was *set* in heaven.

Revelation 4:3 reads, "And he that sat was to look upon like a jasper and a sardine stone: and there was a rainbow round about the throne, in sight like unto an emerald." This is a description of the Ancient of Days with the description of the Son of man (Jesus). Revelation 1:13–18 shows on whom the glory of God rests. Even Revelation 21:22–23 shows on whom the glory rests: "And I saw no temple therein for the

Lord God Almighty and the Lamb are the temple of it. And the city had no need of the sun, neither of the moon, to shine in it: for the glory of God did lighten it, *and the Lamb is the light thereof*" (emphasis added).

There will be twenty-four elders sitting around the throne, twelve on the right-hand side and twelve on the left, with God in the midst. They are glorified human beings representing the redeemed of both the old and new covenants. Who are they? That position is reserved for those whom God the Father prepared beforehand, who would occupy that position (Mark 10:37–40). Note that God Almighty does not have angels sitting next to him but the redeemed sons of men, now exalted into his royal family as sons of God. The songwriter of "At Calvary" says, "Oh the love that drew salvation plan. Oh the grace that bought it down to man. Oh the mighty gulf that God did span at Calvary. Mercy there was great, and grace was free. Pardon there was multiplied to me; there my burdened soul found liberty, at Calvary." Praise the Lord!

The *rainbow* around the throne represents God's nature, expressed in glory around his throne.

We read in Revelation 4:5, "And out of the throne proceeded lightning and thunder and voices; and there were seven lamps of five burning before the throne which are the seven spirits of God." This represents his manifested abilities. See Isaiah 11:1–3.

Revelation 4:6 reads, "And before the throne there was a *sea of glass* like unto crystal" (emphasis added). This description is given to represent the vast area before the throne of God reserved for special worshippers. Who are they? This area will be occupied by Jewish saints who have been saved as a result of the preaching of the 144,000 Jewish evangelists who have a double portion of the anointing of the Holy Ghost that the church will have when it is raptured. They will be saved after the church is raptured, at the time of the Jewish harvest as seen in Revelation 15:2–4. That golden stage will be so pure, it will look like glass.

We read in Revelation 4:6–8, "And round about the throne, were four beasts full of eyes before and behind. And the first beast was like a lion, and the second beast like a calf, and the third beast had a face as a man, and the fourth beast was like a flying eagle. And the four beasts had each of them six wings about him; and they were full of eyes within: and they rest not day and night, saying, Holy, holy, holy, Lord God Almighty, which was, and is, and is to come."

These creatures are the seraphim mentioned in Isaiah 6:1–3. Their responsibility is to worship the beauty of God's holiness. They have eyes to look unto the holiness of God and therefore cannot stop worshipping him with sporadic and spontaneous praise. They give glory to the true and only living God. They were created by Jesus to do just that. "For without him was not anything made that was made" (John 1:3).

Let's take a look at Isaiah 6:1–3: "In the year that king Uzziah died I saw also the Lord sitting upon a throne, high and lifted up, and his train filled the temple. Above it stood the seraphim: each one had six wings; with twain he covered his face, and with twain he covered his feet, and with twain he did fly. And one cried unto another, and said, Holy, holy, holy, is the Lord of hosts: the whole earth is full of his glory."

We see the twenty-four elders worshipping God and casting their crowns before the throne, saying, "Thou art worthy oh Lord to receive glory and honor and power. For thou hast created all things, and for thy pleasure they are and were created."

Let me remind you of this great God, our Lord Jesus Christ. We read in Timothy 6:14–16, "That thou keep this commandment without spot, unrebukeable, until the appearing of our Lord Jesus Christ: Which in his times he shall shew, who is the blessed and only Potentate, the King of kings, and Lord of lords; who only hath immortality, dwelling in the light which no man can approach unto; whom no man hath seen, nor can see: to whom be honor and power everlasting. Amen."

REVELATION CHAPTER 5

Revelation 5:1 reads as follows: "And I saw in the right hand of him that sat on the throne a book written within and on the backside, sealed with seven seals." This book seems to contain in it God's plan of redemption, the contents of which must be executed by a worthy vessel (v. 2–3).

A proclamation and challenge go forth to all humankind as to their suitableness and worthiness to open the book and to loose the seven seals. No person in heaven, not even Enoch or Elijah, the latter of whom who escaped death and were taken to heaven, is worthy to open it—no person on earth is. This means that none of the apostles, not even John the Beloved Disciple, is worthy, nor even Moses, Abraham, or any of the martyrs of Jesus will be found worthy.

"Indeed all have sinned and come short of the glory of God" (Romans 3:23). John wept much as he thought that the hope of humankind's redemption was lost.

Revelation 5:5 reads, "And one of the elders saith unto me, Weep not: behold, the Lion of the tribe of Judah, the Root of David, hath prevailed to open the book, and to loose the seven seals thereof."

Verse 6 reads, "And I beheld, and, lo, in the midst of the throne and of the four beasts, and in the midst of the elders, stood a Lamb as it had been slain, having seven horns and seven eyes, which are the seven Spirits of God sent forth into all the earth." In these few verses mentioned above, the personal pronoun *I* is used often, for example, "and I saw," "and I wept," "and said to me," "and I beheld." John was totally involved in beholding this drama that unfolded right before his very eyes.

The Lamb of God is no ordinary lamb. When John the Baptist first saw Jesus, he said, "Behold the Lamb of God that taketh away the sin of the world" (John 1:29). The Lamb has seven horns and seven eyes. The horns speaks of his perfect power to bring about redemption. When Jesus rose from the dead, he said, "All hail, all power in heaven and in earth is delivered unto me." And Romans 1:4 states, "And declared to be the Son of God with power, according to the spirit of holiness, by the resurrection from the dead." The seven eyes speak of his omniscience. He fulfilled all the righteous demands of a holy God for redemption of humankind's sin.

Hebrews 9:11–12 states, "But Christ being come an high priest of good things to come, by a greater and more perfect tabernacle, not made with hands, that is to say, not of this building. Neither by the blood of goats and calves, but by his own blood he entered in once into the holy place, *having obtained eternal redemption for us*" (emphasis added).

God in his fullness is involved in the work of redemption for us! Colossians 2:9 states, "For in him dwelleth all the fulness of the Godhead bodily."

Matthew 13:44 states, "Again, the kingdom of heaven is like unto treasure hid in a field; the which when a man hath found, he hideth, and for joy thereof goeth and selleth all that he hath, and buyeth that field." Verses 45–46 read, "Again, the kingdom of heaven is like unto a merchant man, seeking goodly pearls. Who, when he had found one pearl of great price, went and sold all that he had, and bought it."

God's response to the kingdom and humankind's response to the kingdom should be to sell out all in order to buy it. We should understand that the kingdom of God is so precious that no sacrifice is too much to give or surrender to purchase it. Are you willing to surrender all to pursue the kingdom? God's response is, "For God so love the world that he gave his only begotten Son that whosoever believeth in him should not perish but have everlasting life."

In Luke 12:32 Jesus says, "Fear not, little flock; for it is your Father's good pleasure to give you the kingdom." Jesus says that humankind's response to the kingdom should be "If any man cometh after me, let him deny himself, take up his cross, and follow me. For whosoever cometh after me and taketh not up his cross is not worthy of me." May God open our eyes to behold the glorious privilege we have to be part of his kingdom, which outshines the sun. Matthew 13:43 reads, "Then shall the righteous shine forth *as the sun* in the kingdom of their Father. Who hath *ears to hear*, let him hear" (emphasis added). Again I repeat: Indeed in Christ dwelleth all the fullness of the Godhead bodily. All of God is involved in the work of redemption to save our souls and to give us the expected end of eternal life.

When the Lamb took the book out of God the Father's hands, the four beasts and the twenty-four elders fell down before the Lamb in worship, having harps and golden vials full of odors, which are the prayers of the saints.

It's time to rejoice, because the prayers of the saints will be answered. They have been stored up in golden vials, and their sweet aroma is about to be released before God. They worship the Lamb of God (Jesus) and sing this song: "Thou are worthy to take the book, and to open the seals thereof: for thou was slain, and hath redeemed us to God by thy blood out of every kindred, and tongue, and people and nations; and hast made us unto our God kings and priests: and we shall reign on the earth" (Revelation 5:9–10).

God indeed will get rid of this evil and wicked form of governance in the world, and the saints of God will reign with him on the earth for one thousand years, after which the wicked dead will be resurrected and judged by God (Revelation 20:11–15), which will be followed by his eternal kingdom that will have no end!

We read in Daniel 7:13–14, "I saw in the night visions, and, behold, one like the Son of man came with the clouds of heaven, and came to the Ancient of days, and they brought him near before him. And there was given him dominion, and glory, and a kingdom, that all people, nations, and languages, should serve him: his dominion is an everlasting dominion, which shall not pass away, and his kingdom that which shall not be destroyed."

Revelation 5:11 reads, "And I beheld, and I heard the voice of many angels round about the throne and the beasts and the elders: and the number of them was ten thousand times ten thousand, and thousands of thousands."

Certainly this number of angels is more than the number of people presently living on Planet Earth. Please remember this figure, because in chapter 7 we will be doing some comparison of the saints who are redeemed.

Revelation 5:12 reads, "Saying with a loud voice, Worthy is the Lamb that was slain to receive power, and riches, and wisdom, and strength, and honour, and glory, and blessing."

Verse 13 reads, "And every creature which is in heaven, and on the earth, and under the earth, and such as are in the sea, and all that are in them, heard I saying, Blessing, and honour, and glory, and power, be unto him that sitteth upon the throne, and unto the Lamb for ever and ever."

Note that the same respect given to the God of the universe is the same respect given to the Lamb (Jesus). They are indeed one.

John 14:8-9 reads, "Philip saith unto him, Lord, shew us the Father, and it sufficeth us. Jesus saith unto him, *Have I been so long time with you, and yet hast thou not known me, Philip? he that hath seen me hath seen the Father; and how sayest thou then, Shew us the Father?*" (emphasis added).

In John 10:30 Jesus says, "I and my Father *are one*" (emphasis added). "And the four beasts said 'Amen,' and the twenty-four elders fell down and worshipped him that liveth forever and ever" (Revelation 5:14).

First Peter 1:3-4 states, "Blessed be the God and Father of our Lord Jesus Christ, which according to his abundant mercy hath begotten us again unto a lively hope by the resurrection of Jesus Christ from the dead. To an inheritance incorruptible, and undefiled, and that fadeth not away, reserved in heaven for you." And let the church say amen!

REVELATION CHAPTER 6

The book that the Lamb of God has in his hand will determine the future and state of the nations and will also determine the future and state of the church of the living God. It will also set the stage for the rapture of the Lamb's purchased bride, along with setting the state for the trumpet judgments. It paves the way for the bride to inherit her heavenly home. The book has the legal right to cleanse the heavenly realm for the bride of Christ to occupy. These statements will be clarified as we go along.

Revelation 6:1 reads, "And I saw when the Lamb opened one of the seals, and I heard, as it were the noise of thunder, one of the four beasts saying, Come and see." John was given the privilege of seeing the effects that the breaking of the seals will have on Planet Earth. It will have the power to changes world politics as it marches forward, toward the battle of Armageddon. The noise of thunder shows the power of the Lamb as he holds the world's future in his hands.

In verse 2, when the first seal is broken, John says, "And I saw, and behold a white horse: and he that sat on him had a bow; and a crown was given unto him: and he went forth conquering, and to conquer."

The Lamb breaks the first seal in heaven, and there is a corresponding action on earth. The Antichrist is released. The Antichrist comes as the hope of the nations. Rebellious man has rejected God and his Christ. They say set Barabbas free (who was a murderer) but who will come to kill/crucify Jesus, the innocent Lamb of God. Jesus said to the Jews, "I came in my Father's name and ye refuse me. Another shall come in his own name, him you will receive." The Antichrist will make a peace covenant with the Jews and the surrounding nations for one week (seven years). But in the midst of the week (three and a half years), he will break his covenant with the Jews. It's at this that their eyes will be opened (Daniel 9:27; Matthew 24:15). The Antichrist is the counterfeit savior that the world is looking for. A crown was given unto him. He will head world politics and will serve as the head of the one world government. He will be the king of the world. He goes forth conquering and to conquer. Whether it's that a two-thirds majority is needed by the nations of the world to give him that power, the other nations will eventually fall under his jurisdiction.

Verses 3–4 read, "And when he had opened the second seal,

I heard the second beast say, Come and see. And there went out another horse that was red and power was given to him that sat thereon to take peace from the earth, and that they should kill one another. And there was given unto him a great sword."

Martial law will be implemented to ensure that the nations of the world comply. The office of the nations of the world will issue an edict that will bring swift judgment on lawbreakers.

Be wise and don't put yourself in undue danger. The time will come in the breaking of the fourth seal when you will have to stand bold for your faith in Jesus and even lose your life for this. I encourage you to do so joyfully and boldly when this time comes.

This second seal introduces martial law. If the authorities say, for example, not to be outdoors after ten o'clock at night and you choose to go out after ten, because you are not a part of the military system, and are shot, then you die by lack of knowledge, but not as a martyr for Jesus. But you will still go to heaven if you are saved.

Verses 5–6 read, "And when he had opened the third seal, I heard the third beast say, Come and see. And I beheld, and lo a black horse; and he that sat on him had a pair of balances in his hand. And I heard a voice in the midst of the four beasts say, A measure of wheat for a penny, and three measures of barley for a penny; and see thou hurt not the oil and the wine."

The time is coming when strict sanctions will be implemented to control the sale and purchasing of goods for consumption. Dark days are ahead for the world economy. The black horse may represent food restrictions; there may be food rationing. The point I want to make is, in light of "A measure of wheat for a *penny* and three measures of barley for a *penny*" (emphasis added), that *money* will be used during the early stages of the Antichrist's rule. Many people say that when the Antichrist comes, we will have to receive a mark of 666 to buy or sell. Well, the compulsory mark will be implemented after the church is raptured (Revelation chapter 13). Therefore don't be deceived once the Antichrist comes on the scene, money is used in the first three and a half years of his reign. It is in the second three and a half years of his seven-year reign that the mark shall be implemented, which we will discuss later.

You may be saying, "But the church will be raptured before the Antichrist comes on the scene." This will be discussed later; just have some patience.

Revelation 6:7–8 reads, "And when he had opened the fourth seal, I heard the voice of the fourth beast say, Come and see. And I looked and behold a pale horse: And his name that sat on him was Death, and hell followed with him. And power was given unto them over the fourth part of the earth, to kill with sword, and with hunger, and with death, and with the beasts of the earth."

Consider this:
The first horse—white
The second horse—red
The third horse—black
The fourth horse—pale

Pale is not a color, yet theologians who have done research on the pale horse say the color that John saw was green. The national colors of my country are red, white, and black. Most countries have different national color schemes. I wonder what your country's color scheme is.

Am I saying that politics will become such that the Antichrist will use a certain degree of political science to martyr true believers in Christ? There will be an ideology of worldwide unity and globalization, and Christians will be regarded as outcasts to this system of governance. An order will be passed to get rid of them. Remember what Haman attempted to do to the Jews in the Bible book of Esther? In that case, the Jews were spared through prayer and fasting. But in this case the saints of God will be given over into the hands of their enemies for persecution and martyrdom—all to the glory of God.

Daniel 7:21 reads, "I beheld, and the same horn made war with the saints, and prevailed against them." This represents the persecution of Christians before the rapture of the church. But there will also be persecution of the saints who are saved after the church is raptured. Daniel 7:25 speaks of this persecution that continues after the church is raptured: "And he shall speak great words against the most High, and shall wear out the saints of the most High, and think to change times and laws: and they shall be given into his hand until *a time and times and the dividing of time*" (emphasis added).

> The time is 1 year times 2 years, and 0.5 times 0.5 year = 1 + 2 + 0.5 = 3.5 years. So you know now that the Antichrist's reign of persecution continues for the last three and a half years of his reign.

Getting back to Revelation, what is your ideology about Jesus, the only Savior of the world? Their ideology leads to death, not to life. They are the haters of Jesus who will be responsible for killing, martyring, the true believers of Jesus during that period. The fourth horse rider will bring a wave of persecution upon the church. Persecution will hit the Western Hemisphere like a thunderbolt. The saints will be tested and tried, and many will be killed for their faith in Jesus.

The modes of killing will be as follows:

- by the sword (or maybe by a bullet)
- with hunger—Christians placed in jail and not fed
- by death (maybe a dead Christian being chained to a living one until death occurs—most horrible)
- by being given to the beasts of the earth (thrown to lions, tigers, etc.)—that which happened in centuries past will repeat itself, but with more severe magnitude.

REVELATION CHAPTER 6

Revelation 6:9–11 reads as follows:

> And when he had opened the fifth seal, I saw under the altar the souls of them that were slain for the

word of God, and for the testimony which they held: And they cried with a loud voice, saying, *How long, O Lord, holy and true, dost thou not judge and avenge our blood on them that dwell on the earth?* And white robes were given unto every one of them; and it was said unto them, that they should rest yet for a little season, until their fellow servants also and their brethren, that should be killed as they were, should be fulfilled. (emphasis added)

This concept works hand in hand with the fourth seal, indicating when Christians will be killed. These saints must join the martyred group of the fourth seal and await the rapture and God's judgment of vengeance upon the wicked. So we can clearly state that up to the time of the breaking of the fifth seal, the church has not been raptured.

Revelation 6:12–17 reads as follows:

And I beheld when he had opened the sixth seal, and, lo, there was a great earthquake; and the sun became black as sackcloth of hair, and the moon became as blood; and the stars of heaven fell unto the earth, even as a fig tree casteth her untimely figs, when she is shaken of a mighty wind. And the heaven departed as a scroll when it is rolled together; and every mountain and island were moved out of their places. And the kings of the earth, and the great men, and the rich men, and the chief captains, and the mighty men, and every bondman, and every free man, hid themselves in the dens and in the rocks of the mountains; and said to the mountains and rocks, Fall on us, and hide us from the face of him that sitteth on the throne, and from the wrath of the Lamb: For the great day of his wrath is come; and who shall be able to stand?

Charles Darwin's theory of evolution is thrown out the window. Rebellious humankind is finally gripped with the fear of God and seeks a hiding place to run from the presence of God. Rebellious humankind does not drop to their knees in repentance but rather runs from God. This is not the demonstration of the wrath of God. The stage is being set. The judgment and the wrath of God are seen executed in the trumpet judgment and the vial judgments. This is the setting of the stage for what is ahead. We all know that God has not appointed the church to wrath. So then before the wrath of God is poured out, we expect the church to be gone.

Note the testimony of the ungodly: "*The day of his wrath* has come." They say that in panic mode. Therefore, what has taken place in the breaking of the previous seals is not the wrath of God, and therefore the church is still around.

Can we know, or are we entitled to know, the deep truth about God's plan in the redemptive process or program? Well, God the Father gave Jesus the facts in the book of Revelation for us to know, enjoy, appreciate, and receive.

"The great day of his wrath has come." Humankind has to acknowledge the supremacy of God one way or another. Jesus says, "Whosoever shall fall on this stone shall be broken, but on whosoever it shall fall, it will grind him to powder" (Matthew 21:44). Will you submit yourself to Jesus in brokenness and allow his life to transform you? Or will you continue to rebel against his authority? Well, Judgment Day is coming, when he will grind you to powder. The haughtiness and pride of humankind will be brought to nothingness.

REVELATION CHAPTER 7

We read in Revelation 7:1, "And after these things I saw four angels standing on the four corners of the earth, holding the four winds of the earth, that the wind should not blow on the earth, nor on the sea, nor on any tree." It is good news to know that God is in control over the entire earthly realm. He dispatched four angels, who have occupied strategic positions. They are seen standing on the four corners of the earth, holding back the wind from blowing. We take many things for granted and often are unthankful to God for the fresh breeze we enjoy every day. Now the wind is motionless. There is a true saying, "It's calm before a storm." God is about to judge this rebellious world for all its atrocities. But there are some unfinished preliminaries that have to happen before he does so.

Verse 2 reads, "And I saw another angel ascending from the east, having the seal of the living God: and he cried with a loud voice to the four angels, to whom it was given to hurt the earth and the sea."

This angel that ascends from the east must have descended earlier. He may have been surprised by the sudden appearance of the four angels who were given power to hurt the earth and the sea. Again, this angel has the seal of the living God and is on a special assignment from God to ensure that the 144,000 Jews are well prepared for the task that lies ahead of them. He cries out to the four angels, saying, "*Hurt not* the earth, neither the sea, nor the trees till we have sealed the servants of our God in their foreheads." He uses the rank of his authority to restrain the four angels from hurting the earth and the sea. He will be of a higher rank than they. Anyone carrying the seal of God must be of extremely high rank. In the book of Esther, remember, Mordecai was promoted next to King Ahasuerus. Esther 8:2 reads, "And the king took off his ring, which he had taken from Haman, and gave it unto Mordecai. And Esther set Mordecai over the house of Haman." The king further instructs Esther the queen and Mordecai the Jew in verse 8: "Write ye also for the Jews, as it liketh you, in the king's name, and seal it with the king's ring: for the writing which is written in the king's name, and sealed with the king's ring, may no man reverse."

Remember in the book of Genesis what Pharaoh did to Joseph when he promoted him next to him? We read as follows in Genesis 41:41–44:

> And Pharaoh said unto Joseph, See, I have set thee
> over all the land of Egypt. And Pharaoh took off his
> ring from his hand, and put it upon Joseph's hand,

and arrayed him in vestures of fine linen, and put a gold chain about his neck. And he made him to ride in the second chariot which he had; and they cried before him, Bow the knee: and he made him ruler over all the land of Egypt. And Pharaoh said unto Joseph, I am Pharaoh, and without thee shall no man lift up his hand or foot in all the land of Egypt.

This is a very important doctrine. The Jews must be sealed with the Holy Ghost before God will bring judgment upon this rebellious world. This angel is highlighted, but he is working alongside several other angels in preparing the 144,000 Jews for the double anointing of what the church has. No general in God's army travels alone. Note the angel said "*Hurt not.*" This means that up to that point in time, God has not initiated the hurt. Neither his judgments nor his wrath has been poured out yet. This also means that because (a) what has been taking place in the breaking of the seals *is not the wrath of God expressed*, and (b) we believe that God has not appointed us to wrath, the church could still be around up to that point! The angel said "hurt not till *we* have sealed." The plural pronoun is used, which suggests that a company of angels are engaged in preparing the 144,000 Jews for the mighty baptism of the Holy Spirit.

REVELATION CHAPTER 7

Revelation 7:4 reads, "And I heard the number of them which were sealed: and there were sealed an hundred and forty and four thousand of all the tribes of the children of Israel." That amounts to twelve thousand from every tribe, which are Judah, Reuben, Gad, Aser, Nephthalim, Manasses, Simeon, Levi, Isacher, Zabulon, Joseph, and Benjamin. I do not know what John heard when they were sealed, but the Bible tells us he heard something. We can make a thousand and one guesses and perhaps not come close to knowing what he heard. I would like to guess what John heard as they were sealed. They may have said, *Alleluia, I have found him whom my soul so long has craved. Jesus satisfied my longing. Through his blood I am made whole. Alleluia.*

The sealing must be looked upon as the Holy Spirit coming upon them. Ephesians 1:13 states, "In whom ye also trusted, after that ye heard the word of truth, the gospel of your salvation: in whom also after that ye believed, ye were *sealed with that Holy Spirit of promise*" (emphasis added).

The 144,000 are now baptized with a double portion of the Holy Spirit. They are harvesters of the Jews and strictly assigned the task of preaching the gospel to their Jewish brothers as God now turns his attention back to the Jews.

The apostle Paul says in Romans 11:15, "For if the casting away of them be the reconciling of the world, what the receiving of them shall be, but life from the dead?" You can read the rest of Romans chapter 11 for more instructive teachings.

In discussing the sealing of the tribes, it must be pointed out that Judah got a promotion. We know that Jesus, according to the seed of David, came from the tribe of Judah. Also, Dan was left out and Manasses took its place. Dan became steeped in idolatry. God hates idolatry. These tribes were sealed simultaneously, but it was written in that way so we would know the Twelve Tribes were sealed.

How and when does this spectacular event occur? This event occurs in harmony with the rapture of the church. How can we prove this statement? Let's go back to Paul's statement in Romans 11:15: "For if the casting away of them be the reconciling of the world, what the receiving of them shall be, but life from the dead?"

God turns his attention back to the Jews. There are gathered twelve thousand from every tribe. What then should you expect to happen to the church—*life from the dead* for the church? Who was Paul addressing when he made that prophetic statement? Romans 1:7 reads, "To all that be in Rome, beloved of God, called to be saints:

Grace to you and peace from God our Father, and the Lord Jesus Christ" ("and to all nations"—Romans 16:26). In other words, Paul was speaking to the church at large. So, when the Jews are gathered, twelve thousand from each tribe, what will happen to the church? "Life from the dead." Life from the dead is the rapture of the church! To make this statement plain, I'll add that we will be caught up to meet the Lord in the air, so we shall ever be with the Lord.

Immediately after the last tribe is sealed, we see the rapture; the saints are caught up in heaven.

Revelation 7:9 reads, "After this I beheld, and, lo, a great multitude, which no man could number, of all nations, and kindreds, and people, and tongues, stood before the throne, and before the Lamb, clothed with white robes, and palms in their hands."

> This is the prophetic fulfillment of Paul's statement in Romans 11:15.

Paul was showing the blessedness of the Jewish people. Their being cast away in unbelief brought salvation to the world. Their receiving will be life from the dead for the church (rapture).

Acts 13:44–49 reads as follows:

> And the next sabbath day came almost the whole city together to hear the word of God. But when the Jews saw the multitudes, they were filled with envy, and spake against those things which were spoken by Paul, contradicting and blaspheming. Then Paul and Barnabas waxed bold, and said, It was necessary that the word of God should first have been spoken to you: but seeing ye put it from you, and judge yourselves unworthy of everlasting life, lo, we turn to the Gentiles. For so hath the Lord commanded us, saying, I have set thee to be a light of the Gentiles, that thou shouldest be for salvation unto the ends of the earth. And when the Gentiles heard this, they

were glad, and glorified the word of the Lord: and as
many as were ordained to eternal life believed. And
the word of the Lord was published throughout all
the region.

Well, who are the Gentiles? Once you are not a Jew, you are
a Gentile regardless of your nationality. If you cannot trace your
bloodline back to Abraham, you are a Gentile. Thanks be to God for
including us in his plan of salvation. In Matthew 1:5, dealing with
the genealogy of Jesus, Ruth, of the Moabites, was included as being
a part of the lineage that produced King David, through which Jesus
later came in the flesh.

Let's go back to this marvelous sealing of the 144,000
Jews and the simultaneous company seen in heaven
that is the rapture of the church.

ALL TRUTHS ARE PARALLEL

It is said that the Old Testament is the New Testament concealed
and that the New Testament is the Old Testament revealed. In 2
Kings 2 we read of the story of Elijah and Elisha. This parallel
that I am about to share is very important to our understanding
of Revelation chapter 7 with regard to the sealing of the 144,000
Jews and the simultaneous company of saints seen in heaven after
they are sealed.

Second Kings 2:9–15 reads as follows:

And it came to pass, when they were gone over, that
Elijah said unto Elisha, Ask what I shall do for thee,
before I be taken away from thee. And Elisha said, I
pray thee, let a double portion of thy spirit be upon
me. And he said, Thou hast asked a hard thing:
nevertheless, if thou see me when I am taken from
thee, it shall be so unto thee; but if not, it shall not

be so. And it came to pass, as they still went on, and talked, that, behold, there appeared a chariot of fire, and horses of fire, and parted them both asunder; and Elijah went up by a whirlwind into heaven. And Elisha saw it, and he cried, My father, my father, the chariot of Israel, and the horsemen thereof. And he saw him no more: and he took hold of his own clothes, and rent them in two pieces. He took up also the mantle of Elijah that fell from him, and went back, and stood by the bank of Jordan; and he took the mantle of Elijah that fell from him, and smote the waters, and said, Where is the Lord God of Elijah? and when he also had smitten the waters, they parted hither and thither: and Elisha went over. And when the sons of the prophets which were to view at Jericho saw him, they said, "The spirit of Elijah doth rest on Elisha." And they came to meet him, and bowed themselves to the ground before him.

The same thing that happened when Elijah was taken to heaven (raptured) and the mantle of Elijah fell on Elisha, who stayed back for ministry among the Jews, is what will happen when the church is raptured. Elisha asked Elijah for a double portion of his spirit. Elijah said, "For this thing to happen to you, you will have to see me being caught up." The double portion is not for the church but is reserved for the 144,000 Jews. God is going to use the power and glory that it takes to rapture the church to fall upon the 144,000 Jews. They are going to have a double portion of the anointing that the church had to go through the final stages of redemption and to win many of their Jewish brothers to Christ during the seventieth week of Daniel's prophecy (Daniel 9:24). I repeat, it's going to be simultaneous. The church is raptured and the Jews (144,000) are sealed. That's why we see, immediately after they are sealed, a great company of believers *in heaven*.

Revelation 7:11–12 reads, "And all the angels stood round about the throne, and about the elders and the four beasts, and fell before the throne on their faces, and worshipped God, saying, amen: blessing, and glory, and wisdom, and thanksgiving, and honour, and power, and might, be unto our God for ever and ever. Amen."

In Revelation 5:11, John gives the number of angels who came round about the throne as 10,000 × 10,000—thousands upon thousands. John surely had a fantastic brain. The number of this group of angels is estimated to be more than the number of people living on Planet Earth, saved as well as unsaved.

Yet when he saw the great multitude of the redeemed from all nations, all kindred, all peoples, and all tongues standing before the throne, saying with a loud voice, "Salvation to our God which sitteth upon the throne, and unto the Lamb," he did not even make an attempt to count them. Instead, he simply said that no person could number them. Certainly this would have included every saint who died from the day of Pentecost to the actual rapture. It would include all the babies, not forgetting those aborted and those killed in the womb by accident or by a malicious act. Never mind all those miscarriages. Wow. It is not the will of God that any such little ones should perish. Remember when Mary was giving her salutation to Elizabeth, who had gotten pregnant six months before her. The babe John the Baptist heard and leaped for joy while in the womb. Luke 1:41 reads, "And it came to pass, that, when Elisabeth heard the salutation of Mary, the babe leaped in her womb; and Elisabeth was filled with the Holy Ghost."

There are those who say that the great multitude in Revelation 7:9–10 are tribulation saints, meaning saints that will be saved during Israel's seventieth week. It is very inconsistent to think that the church had approximately two thousand years to preach the gospel but that when God turns his attention to the Jews to win them to Christ, we see highlighted in Revelation 7:9–10 a countless multitude of Gentiles whom no person could number being saved during Israel's period of harvest. Such people are overly concerned with the statement made in verse 14, which reads, "And I said unto him, Sir, thou knowest, and he said unto me, These are they which came out of *great tribulation*, and have washed their robes and made them white in the blood of the Lamb" (emphasis added).

The church of Jesus Christ has been going through great tribulation from its inception, since the time Steven was stoned, and will be raptured in the fires of tribulation.

Paul says in Acts 14:22, "We must through much tribulation enter the kingdom of God." One must also distinguish the difference between the church's tribulation and Israel's tribulation. Israel's last days of tribulation is not a period of seven years. It is three and a half years after when Israel signs the peace treaty with the Antichrist for seven years. Not having recognized him as a traitor in the first instance, the Israelites will walk hand in hand with him. However, their eyes will be opened when he sets up the abomination of desolation, as spoken of by Daniel the prophet in Daniel 9:27: "And he shall confirm the covenant with many for one week (seven years): and in the *midst of the week* he shall cause the sacrifice and the oblation to cease (three and a half years), and for the overspreading of abominations he shall make it desolate, even until the consummation, and that determined shall be poured upon the desolate." Jesus, quoting the prophet Daniel, said in Matthew 24:15–16, "When ye therefore shall see the abomination of desolation, spoken of by Daniel the prophet, stand in the holy place, (whoso readeth, let him understand:) Then let them which be in Judaea flee into the mountains." When will this happen? In the midst of the week (Daniel 9:27). Jesus went on to say in Matthew 24:21, "For then shall be great tribulation, such as was not since the beginning of the world to this time, no, nor ever shall be."

Jesus identified Israel's great tribulation as being from the time the abomination of desolation is set up to the end of the second three and a half years. So to say that there will be seven years of tribulation is a big mistake. Israel's tribulation will last for three and a half years. It's also called "the time of Jacob's trouble." I repeat, there is no scripture to support a seven-year period of great tribulation. This is a deception. The church, on the other hand, has been going through great tribulation from its inception, and even during the first three and a half years before the rapture, it will continue to go through great tribulation. There is no scripture to show that the church will be raptured at the beginning of Israel's last seven years. The deceptions are so many. The wrath of God will not begin at the beginning of the seven years. All these deceptions are religious dogma that certain theologians want us to swallow. But there is no scripture to support the nexus of their belief systems. So again I say, *Israel enters its seventieth week still blinded*, for had her eyes been opened, she would not have signed the peace covenant with the Antichrist. Israel's eyes are opened in the midst of the seven years, after three and a half years have passed, when the Antichrist will show his real self and set up the abomination of desolation in the Jewish temple.

Psalm 55:20–21 reads, "He hath put forth his hands against such as be at peace with him: he hath broken his covenant. The words of his mouth were smoother than butter, but war was in his heart: his words were softer than oil, yet were they drawn swords."

The book of Psalms says, "He has put forth his hands against such as be at peace with him." Israel will walk in peace with the Antichrist for the first three and a half years. How then are people saying there will be seven years of great tribulation coming to Israel? The Antichrist will break his covenant. When will he break this covenant with Israel? In the midst of the seven years, or three and a half years after the agreement is signed! His words were smoother than butter when he made the agreement, but war was in his heart. Israel got carried away by his great speeches and convincing solutions, but war was in his heart from the beginning. It will come as no surprise— nor will it be a mere change of heart when the Antichrist seeks to destroy them after three and a half years of peace. Believing he has them where he wants them, he will move in for the kill after three and a half years of peace with them. His words in agreeing to the peace were softer than oil, yet were they drawn swords. He will be a great speaker of fair words that will captivate the hearts of many. The Antichrist will persecute the church of Christ for the first period, and after it is raptured he will continue to persecute Israel as a nation and the remnants of its seed.

Revelation 7:17 states, "For the Lamb which is in the midst of the throne shall feed them, and shall lead them unto living fountains of waters: and God shall wipe away all tears from their eyes." The songwriter says it will all be worth it when we see Jesus. All sorrows will soon be erased when we see Christ. One glimpse of his dear face and all sorrows will vanish. So let's faithfully run the race until we see Christ.

Paul says in Romans 8:18, "For I reckon that the sufferings of this present time are not worthy to be compared with the glory which shall be revealed in us." In 2 Corinthians 4:17, he further states, "For our light affliction, which is but for a moment, worketh for us a far more exceeding and eternal weight of glory."

The Lamb in his earthly ministry gave the parable of the prodigal son in Luke chapter 15. When the son returned home from his wanderings, the father said, "Let's kill the fatted calf," signifying that all of God's eternal riches were to be distributed to the saints of the Most High. They would enjoy God and his fullness forever. Let's be merry. Heaven will be an eternal banquet that will never end. The Lamb, who is Jesus, is so rich that he has made provisions to feed the countless multitude of his saints forever and ever. Five loaves and a few fishes in his blessed hands were able to feed more than five thousand men, in addition to the women and children. All tears will be wiped away. It is worth suffering for God now. Weeping may endure for a night, but joy cometh in the morning. Throughout the countless ages of eternity, we will have joy, love, and peace with the praises of God in our hearts and on our lips.

Have you ever considered Ephesians 2:7? "That in the ages to come he might show the exceeding riches of his grace in his kindness toward us through Christ Jesus." The Holy Ghost is saying that God will take the pleasure of unfolding the complete plan of salvation to us. He will show or manifest the exceeding riches of his grace. For want of a better expression, he will go to the *extreme limit of his being*, but because God is a limitless being and his love toward us is *fathomless*, he will use eternity to eternity as a yardstick to measure his infinite love toward us and what he has provided for us to enjoy through Jesus Christ our Lord and beautiful Savior. It will take us the ages to ages to come to enjoy the full expression of his love toward his bride—his wife, the church. In other words, at that time we will fall deeper and deeper in love with God. He will show the *exceeding* riches of his grace in his kindness toward us through Jesus Christ. Again, I say that God will use the expanse of eternity to express his deeper love toward us, as the bride of Christ will be engaged in a divine romance that gets better and better, grows deeper and deeper, and gets sweeter and sweeter, having no end. Saint Paul describes the love of God as beyond understanding. You and I should do everything to ensure that we are recipients of God's great plan.

REVELATION CHAPTER 8

Revelation 8:1–5 reads as follows:

> And when he had opened the seventh seal, there was silence in heaven about the space of half an hour. And I saw the seven angels which stood before God; and to them were given seven trumpets. And another angel came and stood at the altar, having a golden censer; and there was given unto him much incense, that he should offer it with the prayers of all saints upon the golden altar which was before the throne. And the smoke of the incense, which came with the prayers of the saints, ascended up before God out of the angel's hand. And the angel took the censer, and filled it with fire of the altar, and cast it into the earth: and there were voices, and thunderings, and lightnings, and an earthquake.

The breaking of the seventh seal is a gateway for the seven trumpets. So we can say technically that the seven trumpet angels operate in the sphere of the breaking of the seventh seal. We must not therefore see the seven trumpet judgments as separate from the seventh seal. To be more bold, I will say that the seven trumpet judgments are a part of the ambit of the breaking of the seventh seal. When the seventh seal is broken, there will be silence in heaven for half an hour. John will then see the seven angels with trumpets about to sound.

Let's go back a little. When the first seal was broken, the first beast said to John, "Come and see." When the second seal was broken, the second beast said to John, "Come and see," with John adding, "I saw a red horse," and so on. Why when the seventh seal is broken does John say, "I saw seven angels which stood before God and to them were given seven trumpets"—so that we should feel that these events are not part of the breaking of the seventh seal? Therefore, the breaking of the seventh seal is inclusive of the seven trumpet judgments. Whereas we say the rapture takes place between the breaking of the sixth and seventh seals. This we observe by biblical sequence and divine content. But this may not be entirely accurate, because the breaking of the seventh seal may be inclusive of the rapture. This picture will get clearer as we go deeper into the subject matter explained in the discussion of Revelation chapter 10.

Will there be silence in heaven when the church is raptured? No! The saints will be crying out, "Salvation to our God which sitteth upon the throne, and unto the Lamb." The praises of God will be a continuous crescendo of praises. This scene may precede the rapture. Something significant is about to take place that has never happened in heaven before. That not even the seraphins of chapter 4:8 which rest not day nor night saying Holy, Holy, Holy Lord God Almighty which was and is, and is to come will be praising God. There will be complete silence. The reason for this silence will be comprehensively dealt with when we discuss Revelation chapter 10, which I consider to be one of the most intriguing chapters of the book of Revelation.

Note that the prayers of the saints are still to be answered! The angel took the golden censer holding the prayers of the saints and offered it with much incense upon the golden altar that was before the throne. The smoke of the incense, which came with the prayers of the saints, ascended up before God out of the angel's hand. The angel took the censer, filled it with fire of the altar, and cast it into the earth, and then there were voices, thunder and lightning, and an earthquake.

I believe that God has to answer the prayers of the saints. He performed this act so that the prayers of all the saints could be answered. Therefore, this act must take place before the church is raptured. The fragrance of the saints' prayers will come up as a sweet sacrifice before God, which will move God into immediate action. Our prayers are, even so, *Come, Lord Jesus, and take your bride away.*

Revelation 8:7–12 deals with the judgments that will be brought about and will affect the earth adversely. When the first four angels sound, a third of the trees, the green grass, and the creatures of the sea, along with ships, rivers, fountains of waters, the sun, the moon, and the stars, will be affected adversely. I do not wish to spend much time here debating the devastation that will be caused by the judgments of these angels.

I would like to fast-forward to verse 13: "And I beheld, and heard an angel flying through the midst of heaven, saying with a loud voice, *Woe, woe, woe,* to the inhabiters of the earth by reason of the other voices of the trumpet of the *three angels, which are yet to sound!*" (emphasis added).

The last three judgments are designed to affect humankind directly. Woes come to rebellious humankind at the sounding of the *fifth, sixth, and seventh* trumpets.

REVELATION CHAPTER 9

The first four trumpet judgments affect the environment in which humankind lives. The other three trumpet judgments are called woes, and they directly affect and inflict torment upon the people on earth *whose names are not written in the book of life.* The first woe will be brought about when the fifth angel sounds. A star will fall from heaven. The rebellion that took place in heaven was led by a created being named Lucifer, which means bright and shining. He is now known as the devil, Satan, the serpent, or the dragon. These are all nicknames that describe his devious character. Genesis 1:1 records God's creation. It reads thus: "In the beginning God created the heaven and the earth."

But verse 2 records the creation of the earth out of form and in total chaos. "And the earth was without form and void; and darkness was upon the face of the deep. And the spirit of God moved upon the face of the waters." As you read through Genesis chapter 1, you observe that everything that God created was good. So an earth without form and void was not created in that way by God. It is believed that between Genesis chapters 1 and 2 is when the war between God and Lucifer occurred. Lucifer tried to overthrow God; in so doing, the chief worshipper of God became God's enemy. Lucifer persuaded a third of the angels of God to join him in this rebellion, and was cast down. Let's read Luke 10:17–18: "And the seventy returned again with joy, saying, Lord, even the devils are subject unto us through thy name. And he said unto them, I beheld Satan as lightning fall from heaven."

Yes, Jesus was there. He is the I AM of the Old Testament and the Jesus of the new covenant. This rebellion was so traumatic that it destroyed all natural life on Planet Earth and left the earth without form and *void of all life*. So when archaeologists find the remains of past civilizations and the bones of prehistoric animals, this must not surprise you. The Bible, God's book of instructions for us, has summarized all these historical facts in a few words: "And the earth was without form and void." God finds it inappropriate to go into any depth concerning civilization before the creation of humankind. We need to trust God's wisdom. And instead of spending millions or billions of dollars on this type of research, we should focus on what God focuses on. Daniel 12:4 states, "But thou, O Daniel, shut up the words, and seal the book, even to the time of the end: many shall run to and fro, and *knowledge shall be increased*" (emphasis added).

Saint Paul said that in the last days, people will be learning and ever learning *but not coming to the knowledge of the Truth.* Verse 1 speaks of an angel who fell from heaven and to whom was given the key of the bottomless pit. This is not one of the holy angels of God. This is, as the scripture says, *a fallen angel.* He opened the bottomless pit, and there arose a smoke out of the pit, as the smoke of a great furnace, and the sun and the air were darkened by reason of the smoke of the pit. And there came out of the smoke locusts upon the earth, and unto them were given power, as the scorpions of the earth have power. The habitation of these creatures is the bottomless pit. They seem to be a special category of evil forces that were held in their prison cells (the bottomless pit) but are now released for a season of five months to afflict the ungodly. A dreadful description of them and their punitive task is revealed in verses 5–10. In those days, people shall seek death, but death shall flee from them. *That is the first woe!*

As we read in Revelation 9:12, "One woe is past, and behold, there come two woes more hereafter."

Revelation 9:13–14 reads, "And the sixth angel sounded, and I heard a voice from the four horns of the golden altar which is before God, saying to the sixth angel which had the trumpet, Loose the four angels which are bound in the great river Euphrates." Some of these fallen angels are so terrible that God in his wisdom gives them special confinement.

They are now loosed for a season, and you see the immediate effects of their diabolic influence caused, persuading evil people to do their bidding by creating unrest, discontentment, rivalry, death, and destruction on a massive scale. Humankind is like a conduit, either allowing the good to influence them by yielding to God or the bad to influence them by yielding to Satan. But the scripture says in John 3:19, "And this is the condemnation, that light is come into the world, *and men loved darkness rather than light, because their deeds were evil"* (emphasis added).

> Choose ye whom ye will serve. I advise you to choose
> God and his goodness, and live.

The Second Woe

We read the following in Revelation 9:15–21:

> And the four angels were loosed, which were prepared for an hour, and a day, and a month, and a year, for to slay the third part of men. And the number of the army of the horsemen were two hundred thousand thousands and I heard the number of them. And thus I saw the horses in the vision, and them that sat on them, having breastplates of fire, and of jacinth, and brimstone: and the heads of the horses were as the heads of lions; and out of their mouths issued fire and smoke and brimstone. By these three was the third part of men killed, by the fire, and by the smoke, and by the brimstone, which issued out of their mouths. For their power is in their mouth, and in their tails: for their tails were like unto serpents, and had heads, and with them they do hurt. And the rest of the men which were not killed by these plagues yet repented not of the works of their hands, that they should not worship devils, and idols of gold, and silver, and brass, and stone, and of wood: which neither can see, nor hear, nor walk: Neither repented they of their murders, nor of their sorceries, nor of their fornication, nor of their thefts.

This is World War III. Remember, we are reading figurative language. Had John seen the modern war machines we have today, he would not have been able to describe them in words. So God gave him a language to describe the actual destruction that will occur when these modern weapons are used. The effects in the description will bring about the same destruction that will occur. One-third of the world's population will be killed, yet humankind will refuse to turn from their evil deeds to God. Ruthless crimes, murders, the violation of human rights, vicious rapes, sexual immorality, and witchcraft will be the order of the day.

REVELATION CHAPTER 10

Chapter 10 in the book of Revelation is one of the shortest chapters but requires the most detailed investigation. It is one of the most intriguing chapters in this book. Anyone who understands chapter 10 correctly will have a deep insight into the whole book. The book of Revelation is for the most part written in chronological order, but not all the time. Sometimes we have interluding periods and overlapping issues. Unlike with some of the other chapters, you can feel the effects that this gives rise to. For example, in Revelation 8:7, when the first angel sounds, one-third of the trees are burned up. In chapter 10, however, what is taking place is not known by natural observation. It is strictly spiritual but explosively dynamic.

Revelation 10:1–4 reads as follows:

> And I saw another mighty angel come down from heaven, clothed with a cloud: and a rainbow was upon his head, and his face was as it were the sun, and his feet as pillars of fire: and he had in his hand a little book open: and he set his right foot upon the sea, and his left foot on the earth, and cried with a loud voice, as when a lion roareth: and when he had cried, seven thunders uttered their voices. And when the seven thunders had uttered their voices, I was about to write: and I heard a voice from heaven saying unto me, Seal up those things which the seven thunders uttered, and write them not.

Rules of Engagement

Before I go into explaining what we have just read, I need you to understand a military term, *rules of engagement*. I would like to highlight a few examples taken from God's Word as we seek greater enlightenment in comprehending the graphic truths in this chapter that otherwise can easily evade us.

Moses was deep in the desert. God called out to him from the burning bush and told him to take off his shoes because the place he was standing was holy ground. The first thing God did was to establish his holiness, and this affects whatever has to be done in the future. Some people in the occult take off their shoes before they enter their so-called holy place. Their practices are unholy. Whatever they do in that place, even though it looks like sacred, is an abomination unto God. He alone is holy and sets his standards of holiness for us to follow. There is none like unto our God. The very presence of his appearance consecrates a place.

The second thing God did was to ask Moses what he had in his hand. Moses said, "A rod." God told Moses to drop the rod, and as Moses obeyed, the rod became a serpent on the ground. So vicious and lively was that serpent that Moses began to run from it. God told Moses to take it up by the tail. As Moses did so, the serpent became a rod in his hand.

Remember, it was the serpent that beguiled Eve. That was the first rule of engagement. God used that Serpent-like rod to whip all the false gods of Egypt. The magicians of Egypt who had the ability, by way of their evil enchantment, to turn their rods into serpents did so in the presence of Moses and Pharaoh. But Moses's serpent ate up all their serpents. That's an example of rules of engagement. Can you imagine the war that took place with Moses's serpent hissing against the Egyptians' serpents, but the supremacy of God prevailed! God showed his supremacy over evil by using the rules of engagement.

The scripture tells us that Jesus took on the form of sinful flesh to condemn sin in the flesh. Not that his flesh was sinful. He is indeed the bread of life, who came down from heaven to give life unto the world. That is, however, a rule of engagement. Hebrews 2:14 states, "Forasmuch then as the children are partakers of flesh and blood, he also himself likewise took part of the same; that through death he might destroy him that had the power of death, that is, the devil." *Through the rules of engagement, Jesus conquered death, hell, and the devil!*

Hebrews 2:16 reads, "For verily he took not on him the nature of angels; but he took on him the seed of Abraham." That is one of the rules of engagement.

Our beloved Jesus went to the cross to destroy the curse of the cross, "for it is written, Cursed is everyone that is hang on a cross" (Galatians 3:13). The whole purpose of Christ's going to the cross was not only to destroy the curse of the cross but also, as it says in verse 14, so that the blessing of Abraham might come upon the Gentiles through Jesus Christ, that we might receive the promise of the Spirit through faith.

When soldiers put on their camouflage outfits to blend with the environment, that is a form of using one of the rules of engagement.

I remember years ago when Idi Amin of Uganda arrested and captured several Israel soldiers. How did Israel manage to release those soldiers? They sent their soldiers dressed like Ugandan soldiers, entered the camp undetected, and released their captive soldiers. *They looked like the Ugandan soldiers, but their purpose of heart* was different. Many times we judge by the outward appearance, but God judges the heart! With the strategy called rules of engagement, you may take on a form or look like the ungodly in your apparel or operations, but your purpose of heart is different. You may be criticized by your counterparts for your modus operandi, but God knows your heart.

So much for the topic of rules of engagement. I will say no more, lest my Christian brothers and sisters criticize me for being unorthodox at times, but it's all for the glory of God.

In the book of Revelation, you see Jesus taking on various roles and responsibilities. His appearance matches the responsibility or task he has to perform.

In Revelation chapter 1, we see Jesus as the Son of man. We see him as the glorified Savior. We see him as the Alpha and Omega, God, the very God. He is the First and the Last.

In Revelation chapters 2 and 3, we see him as the head of the churches. He is the Redeemer and the instructor of the churches. Jesus is the one who walks in the midst of the churches and the one who holds the seven stars in his hand.

In Revelation chapter 5 we see him as the Lamb of God that taketh away the sin of the world. We see him as the Lion of the tribe of Judah who prevailed by his eternal power. I would like to go back now to Revelation chapter 10, having laid a foundation for a better understanding of this intriguing chapter.

Who is this angel? We have so many clues that we cannot mistake him:

- He is clothed with a cloud, which speaks of his divinity.
- He has a rainbow around his head, which speaks of his deity.
- His face is as if it were the sun, which speaks of his majesty.
- His feet as pillars of fire speak of his righteous nature to judge.
- He has a little book open in his hand. It's the same book the Lamb took from the hand of God in Revelation chapter 5. It is now open because the seven seals have been broken.
- He still has the book in his hand.
- He cries with a loud voice as when a lion roars. He is indeed the Lion of the tribe of Judah.
- When he roared, seven thunders uttered their voices. The heavens and the earth declared the glory of God, and the firmament showed his handiwork. Day unto day he uttered speech, and night unto night he showed knowledge.

I have brought out these points to make it easier for you to recognize him. That angel is Jesus Christ. The seven seals are broken, and he holds the little book open in his hand.

The big question is, why has he taken on the form of an angel?

Here, one of the rules of engagement comes in; the Lord is about to take on the greatest angelic war to finally roust the heavens of all evil and satanic forces. It will be the greatest angelic war of all time. When the church is raptured, the heavenly will be cleansed. The heavenly must be cleansed before the church is raptured. Ephesians chapter 6 says we wrestle "not against flesh and blood but against principalities and powers, against the rulers of the darkness of this world, against spiritual wickedness in heavenly places."

The Lion of the tribe of Judah roars as he is about to devour his prey. When he roars, seven thunders utter their voices. The Lamb is zealous for his bride, whom he purchased with his own blood. Can you imagine these evil principalities occupying the heavenly realm for centuries, thousands of years—who knows how long? From the time they were cast out of heaven, out of the throne room of God, they have felt that the heavenly realm is theirs. They have set up shop and made all kinds of evil devices up there to protect them from being evicted. They wish to claim squatting rights. But the Lamb is zealous for his bride to be with him. When the rapture takes place, we will meet the Lord in the air. We will be up there, not to fight devils and demons, but to enjoy God forever. Remember what happened to Daniel when he was praying and fasting for twenty-one days. The angel Gabriel was sent with the answer to Daniel's prayer on the first day. But the prince of Persia resisted and tried to prevent him from going to Daniel with the answer, and then an angelic war took place for which God had to dispatch Michael, the chief warrior angel of God. Gabriel was able to slip through with the answer. Gabriel said he had to go back and continue the fight. The demonic realms that were governing the Persian empire fought against Gabriel, trying to hinder God's plan and his purpose for his people. This will not happen when the church is raptured. Every devil will be brought under the feet of Jesus, of whom we are partakers and members of his body. Psalm 110 tells us that the Lord said, "Sit thou at my right hand until I make thine enemies thy footstool." Just as the battle of Armageddon will be between God and humankind, the battle being discussed here is between God and the angels.

When the angel roars, seven thunders will utter their voices. These seven thunders will answer the roar of the Lion of the tribe of Judah, attesting to the fact that Jesus is the Creator of the heavenly realm. Whatever God creates, he leaves his signature on his creation. Remember Jesus saying to his disciples and to those around him in the hearing of his voice. If they didn't praise him, then the very stones would cry out and praise him.

Indeed this cry is to attest to the lordship of his creation over the heavens that were occupied by demonic forces. Well, they will try to hold on to their squatting territorial rights. The foundation of the heavens will be shaken.

This will be a serious war. Hebrews 12:26–29 says, "Whose voice then shook the earth: but now he hath promised, saying, Yet once more I shake not the earth only, but also heaven. And this word, yet once more, signifieth the removing of those things that are shaken, as of things that are made, that those things which cannot be shaken may remain. Wherefore we receiving a kingdom which cannot be moved, let us have grace, whereby we may serve God acceptably with reverence and godly fear. For our God is a consuming fire."

This cry as the King of kings comes down to reclaim stolen possessions sparks off the most serious angelic war of all time. Again, I say the Lamb is zealous for his bride, whom he purchased with his own blood, and nothing will stand between him and his bride. It's time for the bride to come home.

For a better understanding of this battle, we need to look at Revelation 12:7–8: "And there was war in heaven: Michael and his angels fought against the dragon; and the dragon fought and his angels, and prevailed not; neither was their place found any more in heaven." The Lord Jesus will take on the form of a divine angelic being and will lead this war to roust the heavens of these demonic forces once and for all so that his bride can be raptured.

The seven thunders testify such deep truths about God and his creation that, militarily speaking, John was forbidden to write.

I do not want to know what those seven thunders uttered. Deuteronomy 29:29 tells us that the things that are secret belong to God. Praise his name. The things that are revealed belong to humankind. My prayer is the prayer of Paul the apostle found in Ephesians 1:17–18: "That the God of our Lord Jesus Christ, the Father of glory, may give unto you the spirit of wisdom and revelation in the knowledge of him: The eyes of your understanding being enlightened; that ye may know what is the hope of his calling, and what the riches of the glory of his inheritance in the saints."

Moving on to Revelation 10:5–6, we read, "And the angel which I saw stand upon the sea and upon the earth lifted up his hand to heaven. And sware by him that liveth for ever and ever, who created heaven, and the things that therein are, and the earth, and the things that therein are, and the sea, and the things which are therein, that there should be time no longer."

In Daniel 12:6–7 we see what appears to be a Christophany, which is an appearance or a nonphysical manifestation of Christ. Traditionally, in the Old Testament, the term refers to a vision of Christ. "And one said to the man clothed in linen, which was upon the waters of the river, How long shall it be to the end of these wonders? And I heard the man clothed in linen, which was upon the waters of the river, when he held up his right hand and his left hand unto heaven, and sware by him that liveth for ever that it shall be for a time, times, and an half; and when he shall have accomplished to scatter the power of the holy people, all these things shall be finished."

Revelation 10:7 reads, "But in the days of the voice of the seventh angel, when he shall begin to sound, *the mystery of God* should be finished, as he hath declared to his servants the prophets" (emphasis added).

What is the mystery of God? Paul writes the following in Ephesians 3:1–11:

> For this cause I Paul, the prisoner of Jesus Christ for
> you Gentiles. If ye have heard of the dispensation
> of the grace of God which is given me to you-ward.
> How that by revelation he made known unto me the

mystery; (as I wrote afore in few words, whereby, when ye read, ye may understand my knowledge in *the mystery of Christ*). Which in other ages was not made known unto the sons of men, as it is now revealed unto his holy apostles and prophets by the Spirit; that the Gentiles should be fellow-heirs, and of the same body, and partakers of his promise in Christ by the gospel: Whereof I was made a minister, according to the gift of the grace of God given unto me by the effectual working of his power. Unto me, who am less than the least of all saints, is this grace given, that I should preach among the Gentiles the unsearchable riches of Christ. And to make all men see what is *the fellowship of the mystery*, which from the beginning of the world hath been hid in God, who created all things by Jesus Christ. To the intent that now unto the principalities and powers in heavenly places might be known by the church the manifold wisdom of God. According to the eternal purpose which he purposed in Christ Jesus our Lord. (emphasis added)

The church is the mystery of God, inclusive of both Jews and Gentiles who are saved in this dispensation.

In light of "but in the days of the voice of the seventh angel," we need to identify who this seventh angel is. Once clue to this is the days of the voice.

Go back a little and read Revelation chapter 8, when the various angels sound, to discover what happened. Take for example verse 10: "And the third angel sounded, and there fell a great star from heaven, burning as it were a lamp, and it fell upon the third part of the rivers, and upon the fountain of waters, and the name of the star is called wormwood, and the third part of the waters became wormwood, and many men died of the waters because they were made bitter."

That angel did not sound for days. It was an event when he

sounded: something happened, so this is also true with the sounding of the voices of the other angels. However, a special phrase is used for this seventh angel: the sound, lasting for days, was accompanied by his voice. Remember, in Revelation 8:13 there are three woes yet to come; each of the last three angels produces a woe. The fifth angel produces a woe when he sounds. The fifth and sixth angels each produce a woe when they sound, and the seventh angel produces a woe when he sounds. We have covered two woes and are now looking for the woe produced by the seventh angel. *This is important.*

It will help us trace the events leading up to the woe so we can identify the seventh angel. Can you locate where this woe is located? Turn to Revelation 12:7–12. It reads thus:

> And there was war in heaven: Michael and his angels fought against the dragon; and the dragon fought and his angels. And prevailed not; neither was their place found any more in heaven. And the great dragon was cast out, that old serpent, called the Devil, and Satan, which deceiveth the whole world: he was cast out into the earth, and his angels were cast out with him. And I heard a loud voice saying in heaven, Now is come salvation, and strength, and the kingdom of our God, and the power of his Christ: for the accuser of our brethren is cast down, which accused them before our God day and night. And they overcame him by the blood of the Lamb, and by the word of their testimony; and they loved not their lives unto the death. Therefore rejoice, ye heavens, and ye that dwell in them. *Woe to the inhabitants of the earth and of the sea! for the devil is come down unto you, having great wrath, because he knoweth that he hath but a short time.* (emphasis added)

This woe occurs after Michael and his angels cast the devil and his angels to the earth and their place is found no more in the heavens. Note that the plural, *heavens,* is used. The battle for the heavens will be won by Michael and his angels, spearheaded by Jesus Christ, who will clothe himself in divine angelic form. Therefore, we can conclude that the seventh angel is Michael the archangel.

The voice being referred to by that statement belongs to Michael the archangel. He is the head warrior angel.

In 1 Thessalonians 4:15–18 we read the following:

> For this we say unto you by the word of the Lord, that we which are alive and remain unto the coming of the Lord shall not prevent them which are asleep. For the Lord himself shall descend from heaven with a shout, *with the voice of the archangel,* and with the trump of God: and the dead in Christ shall rise first: Then we who are alive and remain shall be caught up together with them in the clouds, to meet the Lord in the air: and so shall we ever be with the Lord. Wherefore comfort one another with these words. (emphasis added)

The scripture tells us that when Jesus returns to rapture the church, he will be coming with the voice of the archangel (Michael), which indicates, as we said previously, that when the Lord returns for his bride, it will be a time of great battles in the heavens. Jesus will lead and head up the angelic army with a cloud over him and a rainbow around his head as he marshals the angelic host. Rules of engagement! Remember, the Lord speaks and galaxies are formed. He says "Let there be," and there appears whatever he declares. He opens his mouth and planets are formed. There is none like him among the sons and daughters of the Almighty. Yet he comes with the voice of the archangel signaling a time of great spiritual war.

We read the following in Daniel 12:1–3:

> And at that time shall Michael stand up, the great prince which standeth for the children of thy people:

and there shall be a time of trouble, such as never was since there was a nation even to that same time: and at that time thy people shall be delivered, every one that shall be found written in the book. And many of them that sleep in the dust of the earth shall awake, some to everlasting life, and some to shame and everlasting contempt. And they that be wise shall shine as the brightness of the firmament; and they that turn many to righteousness as the stars for ever.

We have established that the seventh angel is Michael. Can you say "Praise the Lord" and give him the glory for such a revelation! This revelation should trickle through your whole theology in relation to the timing of the rapture.

Again we turn to "But in the days of the voice" (Revelation 10:7). Jesus's voice of war continues for a projected period of time, which seems to indicate that this warrior angel and his host will be battling for many days. Furthermore, the chronological record of the first angel through to the seventh angel sounding their trumpets may not necessarily be true in trying to understand this event. Why do I say so? Because the scripture says that when he *shall begin* to sound, the mystery of God should be finished, meaning that when he begins to sound, the church should be raptured. So it means that after the church is raptured, he will continue to sound. For in the *days* of his voice, he will continue to fight even after the church is raptured.

So one can conclude as the war for the heavens rages, the forces of darkness are pushed back and lose ground. The church is raptured as that part of the heavens is cleansed. Remember, Jesus raptures the church with the voice of the archangel, indicating that the battle is not yet over. The battle continues until the time the devil's last resistance is broken, he is routed out of the heavens with his demonic hosts, and he is cast down to the earth. The church is nowhere to be found on earth! So he goes about making war with the remnant of its seed. No human being knows how large the heavens are—that area of real estate will be contested—but we do know that the battle will last for several days. I am suggesting that the battle rages on behind the scenes, the trumpet angels being in the forefront. So by the time the Lion of the tribe of Judah roars and the seven thunders utter their voices, the battle has begun. And this battle began when the seventh seal was broken.

When the seven thunders utter their voices, it indicates who is the Creator and owner of the real estate, which sparks the angelic war for the property.

The terrible thing is that the defeated host of the devil is cast down to the earth, which is a point to note. This battle for the heavens is strictly spiritual and cannot be observed by natural means, for example, by the trees being burned up or the waters being turned to blood.

So that while the trumpet angels are sounding and natural effects are occurring, the battle for the heavens will be raging unseen and unbeknown to humankind. But its dynamic effects will allow the rapture to take place in the cleansing of the heavens and the glorious establishment of the kingdom of God.

When Will the Rapture Take Place?

It is important to note that the apostle Paul, in his writings to the Corinthians, says in 1 Corinthians 15:51–52 that the church will be raptured at the last trumpet. The church is called "the mystery of God" in Ephesians chapter 3. We are working with information that God has given to us. The rapture will take place, not at the first trumpet, and not at the second or third trumpet, but at the last trumpet. In Revelation 10:7 we see a parallel scripture: "In days of the voice of the seventh trumpet angel the mystery of God should be completed." There are seven trumpet angels seen in Revelation chapter 8. It is when the seventh trumpet angel begins to sound that the church will be raptured. This means that the church will go through the trumpet judgments.

Revelation 10:8–11 reads as follows:

And the voice which I heard from heaven spake unto me again, and said, Go and take the little book which is open in the hand of the angel which standeth upon the sea and upon the earth. And I went unto the angel, and said unto him, Give me the little book. And he said unto me, Take it, and eat it up; and it shall make thy belly bitter, but it shall be in thy mouth sweet as honey. And I took the little book out of the angel's hand, and ate it up; and it was in my mouth sweet as honey: and as soon as I had eaten it, my belly was bitter. And he said unto me, Thou must prophesy again before many peoples, and nations, and tongues, and kings.

The seals are broken and the rapture has taken place, but there is another leg to the prophetic testimony of Jesus: the Jews have to get the gospel. The gospel will be spread to the Jewish population by the 144,000 Jewish evangelists, and they will receive it and believe it. The promises are so sweet and the future so bright, but the trials they will have to go through will be very bitter. Not only will this be so, but also the testimonies of the saved ones will bear witness to kings, nations, tongues, and many peoples. And the saved will be tried for their faith.

We read in Daniel 12:10, "Many shall be purified, and made white, and tried; but the wicked shall do wickedly: and none of the wicked shall understand; but the wise shall understand."

REVELATION CHAPTER 11

In Revelation 11:1–2, we read, "And there was given me a reed like unto a rod: and the angel stood, saying, Rise, and measure the temple of God, and the altar, and them that worship therein. But the court which is without the temple leave out, and measure it not; for it is given unto the Gentiles: and the holy city shall they tread under foot forty and two months."

When the abomination of desolation is set up by the Antichrist in the Jewish temple, he shall make an unholy alliance with the nations and shall seek to wipe Israel off the globe. He shall set himself up as God, and the Gentiles will once more possess the land of Israel, for forty-two months, equal to three and a half years.

Revelation 11:3–5 reads, "And I will give power unto my two witnesses, and they shall prophesy a thousand two hundred and threescore days, clothed in sackcloth. These are the two olive trees, and the two candlesticks standing before the God of the earth. And if any man will hurt them, fire proceedeth out of their mouth, and devoureth their enemies: and if any man will hurt them, he must in this manner be killed."

God is going to supernaturally empower his two Last Day prophets to the Jews with an extraordinary anointing to enable them to withstand those who would oppose the ministry of reconciliation and judgment that God has put within their power to perform.

This modern age is filled with high-tech weapons of all types and descriptions. Yet none of these weapons will have any effect on these two prophets of God. If anyone tries to hurt them or kill them, fire will proceed out of their mouths and devour their enemies.

In 2 Kings 1, we read that the king of Samaria sent a captain of fifty soldiers with his fifty to arrest Elijah twice, but Elijah said, "If I be a man of God let fire come down from heaven and consume me and thy fifty"—and it happened. The third captain begged Elijah to spare his life, and the fifty soldiers who were sent with him were speared. Elijah obeyed the instruction from the angel of the Lord.

You see, God can do anything. God will send his two special prophets to testify during the time of the reign of the Antichrist to perform his mission of testifying to the rebellious world, which must be accomplished. The two prophets will be empowered and equipped for the task.

Revelation 11:6 reads, "These have power to shut heaven, that it rain not in the days of their prophecy: and have power over waters to turn them to blood, and to smite the earth with all plagues, as often as they will."

Some theologians allude to the idea that the two prophets are Moses and Elijah. When you look at the miracles they will do, you see that they are similar to the miracles they performed in the Old Testament era. Also they were the two persons who appeared with Jesus on the Mount of Transfiguration.

It is interesting that the last book of the Old Testament, Malachi, mentions both Moses and Elijah. Malachi 4:4–6 states, "Remember ye the law of Moses my servant, which I commanded unto him in Horeb for all Israel, with the statutes and judgments. Behold, I will send you Elijah the prophet before the coming of the great and dreadful day of the Lord: and he shall turn the heart of the fathers to the children, and the heart of the children to their fathers, lest I come and smite the earth with a curse."

This scripture shows that apart from the judgments that they will proclaim, they will reestablish the moral and spiritual values needed to serve God truly and faithfully.

There are other theologians who feel that the two prophets will be Enoch and Elijah as they were the only two persons who never died. This concept is not as strong as the former, although Enoch gave a revelation of the last days.

Jude 1:14–15 reads, "And Enoch also, the seventh from Adam, prophesied of these, saying, Behold, the Lord cometh with ten thousands of his saints, to execute judgment upon all, and to convince all that are ungodly among them of all their ungodly deeds which they have ungodly committed, and of all their hard speeches which ungodly sinners have spoken against him."

Enoch got a glimpse of the battle of Armageddon. We read in Revelation 19:14, "And the armies which were in heaven followed him upon white horses, clothed in fine linen, white and clean. And out of his mouth goeth a sharp sword, that with it he should smite the nations: and he shall rule them with a rod of iron: and he treadeth the winepress of the fierceness and wrath of Almighty God."

> Turning to Revelation 11:7–8, we read, "And when they shall have finished their testimony, the beast that ascendeth out of the bottomless pit shall make war against them, and shall overcome them, and kill them. And their dead bodies shall lie in the street of the great city, which spiritually is called Sodom and Egypt, where also our Lord was crucified."

The beast makes war against these two prophets, whom he will regard as enemies to the state of the united brotherhood. Even though these two prophets of God will have the power to kill those who oppose them, the Antichrist will kill them. I would like to make a wild guess and allow my imagination to run away for a while. Let's say that the Antichrist comes with a battalion of soldiers. The battle begins. Every soldier accompanying the Antichrist is killed, even his special forces. The last man left standing is the Antichrist, who will face off against the two prophets of God. Fire constantly comes out of their mouths. He then kills the two prophets of God as that is their only defense in battle.

Wow! What lessons can we learn from this encounter?

Revelation 13:3–12 mentions that the Antichrist's deadly wound was healed. But there is a difference in verse 3, where we read, "And I saw one of his heads as it were wounded to death; and his deadly wound was healed: and all the world wondered after the beast." This statement may be looked upon as the revival of a previous dominion or empire. But verse 12 states, "And he exerciseth all the power of the first beast before him, and causeth the earth and them which dwell therein to worship the first beast, *whose deadly wound was healed*" (emphasis added). This description shows that he will be killed somewhere around the middle of the seven years of his reign, that is, about three and a half years into that period. He will be resurrected, but not by God's power. Many will disagree with this concept and will say it's only God who can give life. It's true that God is the Author of life. But what God showed me is that when evil reaches a certain level of potency, it can reproduce itself. The Antichrist's deadly wound will be healed, believe it or not, but not by God! When he comes back to life, he will come back as an immortal soul unable to die, one that can live on forever and ever. That's why the two prophets of God will not be able to kill him. He mimics Jesus but is the false messiah.

Revelation 13:4 reads, "And they worshipped the dragon which gave power unto the beast: and they worshipped the beast, saying, Who is like unto the beast? who is able to make war with him?"

The two prophets make war with the Antichrist, but he kills them. Now he feels that he is God and cannot be killed. He cannot die. He sets himself up as God and demands worship. He does not set himself up as God like a madman. The world does not worship him as mad people. But he sets up himself as God because he has gained immortal status. The world will worship him because they realize his immorality.

Second Thessalonians 2:9–12 states, "Even him, whose coming is after the working of Satan with all power and signs and lying wonders, and with all deceivableness of unrighteousness in them that perish; because they received not the love of the truth, that they might be saved. And for this cause God shall send them strong delusion, that they should believe a lie: That they all might be damned who believed not the truth, but had pleasure in unrighteousness."

The Bible says that even though he demands worship, the Antichrist is a man, and his number is 666. He is not God! When the Lord Jesus returns, he will destroy the Antichrist's body and cast him into flaming fire. I imagine the Lord will destroy his body first before casting him into the lake of fire alive!

Daniel 7:11 reads, "I beheld then because of the voice of the great words which the horn spake: I beheld even till *the beast was slain, and his body destroyed, and given to the burning flame*" (emphasis added). *God has to destroy the evil immortal status of the Antichrist's body before casting him into the burning lake of fire.*

Revelation 19:20 reads, "And the beast was taken, and with him the false prophet that wrought miracles before him, with which he deceived them that had received the mark of the beast, and them that worshipped his image. These both were cast alive into a lake of fire burning with brimstone."

Even though The Antichrist's body was destroyed, he was cast alive into the lake of fire burning with brimstone.

Revelation 11:9–10 reads, "And they of the people and kindreds and tongues and nations shall see their dead bodies three days and an half, and shall not suffer their dead bodies to be put in graves. And they that dwell upon the earth shall rejoice over them, and make merry, and shall send gifts one to another; because these two prophets tormented them that dwelt on the earth."

Humankind's response to God's punishment or chastisement is not repentance but rebellion. Unrepentant sinners rejoice when God's two prophets are killed. They even send gifts to one another. It's like saying "Good riddance!"

Revelation 11:11–12 reads, "And after three days and an half the Spirit of life from God entered into them, and they stood upon their feet; and great fear fell upon them which saw them. And they heard a great voice from heaven saying unto them, Come up hither. And they ascended up to heaven in a cloud; and their enemies beheld them."

The world is glued in upon dead bodies of the two prophets. Adverse comments are made. The Antichrist is hailed as the greatest warrior of all time. Pages upon pages are written in exaltation of the beast as the world rejoices over the death of the two prophets of God. Then all of a sudden God steps in. The Spirit of life from God enters into them, and they hear a great voice from heaven saying, "Come up hither." The world is in total shock. The party is over. God then makes swift judgment.

Revelation 11:13 reads, "And the same hour was there a great earthquake, and the tenth part of the city fell, and in the earthquake were slain of men seven thousand: and the remnant were affrighted, and gave glory to the God of heaven." In this case, the rebellious are forced to acknowledge the supremacy of God.

Verse 14 reads, "The second woe is past; and, behold, the third woe cometh quickly." After the first woe passes, all the judgments that follow after this point are all part of the second woe.

We read in verses 15–17, "And the seventh angel sounded; and there were great voices in heaven, saying, the kingdoms of this world are become the kingdoms of our Lord, and of his Christ; and he shall reign for ever and ever. And the four and twenty elders, which sat before God on their seats, fell upon their faces, and worshipped God, saying, We give thee thanks, O Lord God Almighty, which art, and was, and art to come; because thou hast taken to thee thy great power, and hast reigned." This is like a pre-summary of the effects of the sounding of the seventh angel. It is at the sounding of the seventh angel when we hear of the collapse of the kingdoms of this world. This can only happen through warfare. The devil will never give up the kingdoms of this world without a fight. The seventh angel, which in our previous studies has been identified as Michael, will be used by God and ultimately will be led by Jesus, clad in divine angelic form, to usher in the kingdom of God.

Daniel 7:26–27 reads, "But the judgment shall sit, and they shall take away his dominion, to consume and to destroy it unto the end. And the kingdom and dominion, and the greatness of the kingdom under the whole heaven, shall be given to the people of the saints of the most High, whose kingdom is an everlasting kingdom, and all dominions shall serve and obey him."

> We read in Revelation 11:18–19, "And the nations were angry, and thy wrath is come, and the time of the dead, that they should be judged, and that thou shouldest give reward unto thy servants the prophets, and to the saints, and them that fear thy name, small and great; and shouldest destroy them which destroy the earth."

The nations of this world will realize that it is God who pushes the draft knobs. He is in control and determines the destiny of humankind. They nevertheless have a choice to choose God or reject him. Rejecting God has dire consequences. There will be a time for the resurrection of the righteous dead and a time for the resurrection of the wicked dead.

We read in John 5:28–29, "Marvel not at this: for the hour is coming, in the which all that are in the graves shall hear his voice, and shall come forth; they that have done good, unto the resurrection of life; and they that have done evil, unto the resurrection of damnation."

When the wrath of God has come, the seven angels in Revelation chapter 16 will pour out the vials of his wrath upon rebellious humankind. But while God is pouring out his judgments and wrath upon the earth, he will be rewarding his saints in heaven.

Romans 14:10–12 reads, "But why dost thou judge thy brother? or why dost thou set at nought thy brother? for we shall all stand before the judgment seat of Christ. For it is written, As I live, saith the Lord, every knee shall bow to me, and every tongue shall confess to God. So then every one of us shall give account of himself to God."

We read in 1 Corinthians 3:13–15, "Every man's work shall be made manifest: for the day shall declare it, because it shall be revealed by fire; and the fire shall try every man's work of what sort it is. If any man's work abide which he hath built thereupon, he shall receive a reward. If any man's work shall be burned, he shall suffer loss: but he himself shall be saved; yet so as by fire."

Revelation 11:19 reads, "And the temple of God was opened in heaven, and there was seen in his temple the ark of his testament: and there were lightnings, and voices, and thunderings, and an earthquake, and great hail."

Psalm 19:7–11 reads, "The law of the Lord is perfect, converting the soul: the testimony of the Lord is sure, making wise the simple. The statutes of the Lord are right, rejoicing the heart: the commandment of the Lord is pure, enlightening the eyes. The fear of the Lord is clean, enduring forever: the judgments of the Lord are true and righteous altogether. More to be desired are they than gold, yea, than much fine gold: sweeter also than honey and the honeycomb. Moreover by them is thy servant warned: and in keeping of them there is great reward."

REVELATION CHAPTER 12

Revelation 12:1 reads, "And there appeared a great wonder in heaven; a woman clothed with the sun, and the moon under her feet, and upon her head a crown of twelve stars." This woman represents Israel as a nation. She is clothed with the sun and the moon under her feet. It is the God of heaven who has raised up the nation of Israel to be a people unto him. There is no nation like Israel, which was given the oracles of God and was a nation governed by God. When the Israelites went astray, God punished and disciplined them so that they would return unto him. The infinite purposes of God for humanity under the whole of heaven rests upon God's plan and purpose for Israel. He called Israel his inheritance (Psalm 78). The book of Psalms is filled with good examples of how God regards and deals with his people. Romans 3:1–2 states, "What advantage then hath the Jew? or what profit is there of circumcision? Much every way: chiefly, because that unto them were committed the oracles of God."

In Revelation 12:1, the woman in this form has a crown of twelve stars. God has created Israel as a royal crown of diadems. The twelve stars represent the Twelve Tribes through which the Christian community is engrafted. We read in Romans 11:16–19, "For if the first fruit be holy, the lump is also holy: and if the root be holy, so are the branches. And if some of the branches be broken off, and thou, being a wild olive tree, wert grafted in among them, and with them partakers of the root and fatness of the olive tree; boast not against the branches. But if thou boast, thou bearest not the root, but the root thee. Thou wilt say then, The branches were broken off, that I might be grafted in."

Revelation 12:2 reads, "And she being with child cried, travailing in birth, and pained to be delivered."

The enemy of righteousness always challenges the plan of God. But God always has a counterplan to the devil's plan. Remember what happened to the children of Israel in the land of Egypt and how Pharaoh tried to kill all the male babies, but God raised up a deliver in Moses in Pharaoh's own house! Pharaoh paid Moses's mother for taking care of her own son. He was trained and schooled in all the learning of the Egyptians for free. And then God used that same Moses to bring deliverance to the children of Israel who were under Egyptian bondage.

Our God, the God of Abraham, Isaac, and Jacob, is supreme as the God of gods and Lord of lords. He does what he chooses to do under the whole of heaven, and no one can withstand him. When he is angry, he can use the very ones who rebel against him to establish his divine purpose.

Remember what Herod did when Jesus was born, how he killed all the male children two years of age and younger according to the time he had been told by the wise men, when asked, of the birth of Jesus. The devil always tries to destroy God's plan, but God is always ahead of him.

We read in Revelation 12:3–4, "And there appeared another wonder in heaven; and behold a great red dragon, having seven heads and ten horns, and seven crowns upon his heads. And his tail drew the third part of the stars of heaven, and did cast them to the earth: and the dragon stood before the woman which was ready to be delivered, for to devour her child as soon as it was born."

God reminds us that the old enemy of God has no changes to make even though he failed in his attempt to overthrow God. He relentlessly opposed all of God's plan and the plan of redemption. The stars in this case represent the army of rebellious angels who joined him in their mission impossible. This same archenemy of God uses human beings to carry out his evil agenda. In the previous case, he infused Herod and his men of war. Please don't allow him to use you! Set your heart aright and love God. Give no place to the devil. Resist the devil and he will flee from you; draw nigh to God and he will draw nigh to you.

We read in Revelation 12:5, "And she brought forth a man child, who was to rule all nations with a rod of iron: and her child was caught up unto God, and to his throne."

This man-child is Jesus Christ of Nazareth. He will soon take up his rightful position and rule all nations.

Daniel 2:44 states, "And in the days of these kings shall the God of heaven set up a kingdom, which shall never be destroyed: and the kingdom shall not be left to other people, but it shall break in pieces and consume all these kingdoms, and it shall stand for ever." Jesus shall reign over the kingdoms of this world and shall set all things in order. He is the lily of the valley, the Rock of ages, and the bright and morning star.

The rod represents Jesus's right to rule the heathen nations in supreme authority when he returns at the battle of Armageddon. Revelation 19:15 states, "And out of his mouth goeth a sharp sword, that with it he should smite the nations: and he shall rule them with a rod of iron: and he treadeth the winepress of the fierceness and wrath of Almighty God."

> We read in Acts 1:9–11, "And when he had spoken these things, while they beheld, he was taken up; and a cloud received him out of their sight. And while they looked steadfastly toward heaven as he went up, behold, two men stood by them in white apparel; which also said, Ye men of Galilee, why stand ye gazing up into heaven? this same Jesus, which is taken up from you into heaven, shall so come in like manner as ye have seen him go into heaven."

Revelation 12:6 reads, "And the woman fled into the wilderness, where she hath a place prepared of God, that they should feed her there a thousand two hundred and threescore days."

This incident will take place when the Antichrist sets up the abomination of desolation in the holy temple of God, calls himself God, and demands that the world worship him.

In Matthew 24:15–16 Jesus says, "When ye therefore shall see the abomination of desolation, spoken of by Daniel the prophet, stand in the holy place, (whoso readeth, let him understand:) Then let them which be in Judaea flee into the mountains." God has provided a place in the mountains for Israel to flee and be fed for three and a half years.

Revelation 12:7–8 reads, "And there was war in heaven: Michael and his angels fought against the dragon; and the dragon fought and his angels, and prevailed not; neither was their place found any more in heaven."

The heavens are still occupied by the forces of evil. This will soon come to an end at the battles of all battles. The most severe battle of angelic forces will take place to dislodge the devil, nicknamed "the dragon," and his evil angels. It will be the mother of all angelic battles. All the forces of the devil will be summoned to this battle, which will last for days. There will be none like it. As we pointed out when discussing Revelation chapter 10, the angel that roars like a lion and holds the little book in his hand is Jesus—the Lion of the tribe of Judah. He roars to reclaim all stolen territories (the territories of the heavens) that have been occupied by these evil forces for thousands of years or even hundreds of thousands of years. They are coveted territories in which the devil has built his headquarters. These territories are now contested as the Creator of the universe reclaims them. He takes on the form of a divine angel, the only one of its kind, and leads Michael in this decisive battle as he battles for his bride to come home.

We will meet the Lord in the air, but this cannot happen until the heavens are cleansed. You see what happened when God sent Gabriel in answer to Daniel's prayer. It caused an angelic battle that lasted for more than twenty-one days. The angel Gabriel slipped through with the answer to the question "Knowest thou wherefore I come unto thee?" To this he added, "Soon will I return to fight with the prince of Persia: and when I am gone forth, lo, the prince of Grecia shall come." This shows that the battle will continue beyond the twenty-one days. The devil and his demons will be routed from the heavens. They will lose the territorial battle, and the heavens will be finally cleansed.

Revelation 12:9–10 reads, "And the great dragon was cast out, that old serpent, called the Devil, and Satan, which deceiveth the whole world: he was cast out into the earth, and his angels were cast out with him. And I heard a loud voice saying in heaven, Now is come salvation, and strength, and the kingdom of our God, and the power of his Christ: for the accuser of our brethren is cast down, which accused them before our God day and night."

There is a serious attempt by the devil to block our prayers from being heard and answered by God. The mention of night and day would seem to suggest a ceaseless attack and attempt by Satan to hinder the good purposes of God for his church. But thanks be to God, it will soon be over.

I would like, however, to leave you with a word of caution. We need to be careful, and be loving and kind to our fellows. We must demonstrate the spirit of forgiveness among ourselves. As God, for Christ's sake, forgave us, so ought we forgive one another.

Let me give you an example as to how the devil can try to hinder our prayers from being answered. Let's say someone did you wrong and you are holding this person in your heart, unwilling to forgive him or her. When you make your petitions before God, the devil will object to God to try to keep him from granting you that request. He will even be a preacher before God, reminding him of his Word, for example, "God you said if I do not forgive men their trespasses, neither will God forgive me." He will remind God of his Word to prevent your prayers from being answered.

So let's forgive, love, and be obedient to God's Word so that the devil's attempts to block our prayers to God and our blessings from God will have no root or substance.

Revelation 12:11 reads, "And they overcame him by the blood of the Lamb, and by the word of their testimony; and they loved not their lives unto the death."

The precious blood of Jesus Christ delivers us from the scourge of the devil and makes us overcomers. The saints overcome by (1) the blood of the Lamb and (2) by the Word of their testimony. You and I are overcomers by believing in our hearts the redemption message of salvation and making open confession of our faith even if it costs us our lives. We will testify that Jesus Christ is Lord to the glory of God.

Second Corinthians 4:13 states, "We having the same spirit of faith, according as it is written, I believed, and therefore have I spoken; we also believe, and therefore speak."

Romans 10:9–10 says, "That if thou shalt confess with thy mouth the Lord Jesus, and shalt believe in thine heart that God hath raised him from the dead, thou shalt be saved. For with the heart man believeth unto righteousness; and with the mouth confession is made unto salvation."

So God is looking for a heart to believe him and a mouth to speak what the heart believes. Our salvation is based on the finished work at Calvary. But we must believe and confess. It's a heart and mouth business.

Mark 11:22–24 says, "And Jesus answering saith unto them, Have faith in God. For verily I say unto you, That whosoever shall say unto this mountain, Be thou removed, and be thou cast into the sea; and shall not doubt in his heart, but shall believe that those things which he saith shall come to pass; he shall have whatsoever he saith. Therefore I say unto you, What things soever ye desire, when ye pray, believe that ye receive them, and ye shall have them."

Revelation 12:12 reads, "Therefore rejoice, ye heavens, and ye that dwell in them. Woe to the inhabitants of the earth and of the sea! for the devil is come down unto you, having great wrath, because he knoweth that he hath but a short time."

"Rejoice, ye heavens and ye that dwell in them": The heavens are cleansed, the church is in heaven, and it is a significant time to rejoice.

"Woe to the inhabitants of the earth": *This is the third woe.* It comes about by the defeat of the dragon and his angels. They are cast down to the earth itself. The battle is won by Jesus leading the heavenly host of angels in a triumphant victory. *The inhabitants of the earth are now to face the fierce wrath of the devil and his evil angels.* Wow! What a time to live in! Please live a godly life. Don't miss the rapture. If you do, you will be exposed to unimaginable trials and hardship. If you cannot now run with the footmen, how will you be able to run with the horsemen? If you cannot now serve God faithfully in a time of relative peace, how will you be able to serve God in a time of war?

Revelation 12:13-14 reads, "And when the dragon saw that he was cast unto the earth, he persecuted the woman which brought forth the man child. And to the woman were given two wings of a great eagle, that she might fly into the wilderness, into her place, where she is nourished for a time, and times, and half a time, from the face of the serpent."

The woman (Israel) is given two wings like an eagle so that she might fly into the wilderness, to her place where she will be nourished. There are those theologians who say the United States will come to the rescue of the Jews at this critical moment and will fly Israel into the wilderness prepared by God. They say so because the eagle is the symbol of the United States. I do not believe in this interpretation. I believe God will intervene and will supernaturally cause hundreds of thousands of Jews to escape the grip of the Antichrist. Those who seek to flee will be given supernatural help from above to escape the wrath of the Antichrist. Jesus said in Matthew 24:17-18, "Let him which is on the housetop not come down to take anything out of his house: Neither let him which is in the field return back to take his clothes."

> We read in 1 Kings 18:45-46, "And it came to pass in the mean while, that the heaven was black with clouds and wind, and there was a *great rain* and Ahab rode, and went to Jezreel. And the *hand of the Lord was on Elijah*; and he girded up his loins, and ran before Ahab to the entrance of Jezreel" (emphasis added). Imagine a man running faster than a horse to get away from *the great rain*. In a similar way, the hand of the Lord will be upon the Jews as they run to the mountains for safety! It is not the United States coming to their rescue!

In other words, don't even go back home and look for your passport! The instruction from the Master is to flee, to run to the mountains! "When you obey me, I will cause you to run faster than a horse!"

In the mountains, Israel—the Jews—will be nourished for a time (one year), times two (two years) and a half (half a year), which equals three and a half years from facing the serpent.

Revelation 12:15–16 reads, "And the serpent cast out of his mouth water as a flood after the woman, that he might cause her to be carried away of the flood. And the earth helped the woman, and the earth opened her mouth, and swallowed up the flood which the dragon cast out of his mouth."

The spiritual forces of darkness will operate in the legislative counsels of humankind. Laws will be passed like a flood to exterminate Israel and to make Christianity an outlawed religion, punishable by death to those who practice it. To testify about Jesus will mean death. To be caught with a Bible will mean death. Revelation 20:4 reads, "And I saw thrones, and they sat upon them, and judgment was given unto them: and I saw the souls of them that were *beheaded for the witness of Jesus, and for the word of God, and which had not worshipped the beast, neither his image, neither had received his mark upon their foreheads, or in their hands*; and they lived and reigned with Christ a thousand years" (emphasis added). Again I say that laws will be passed in a flood to exterminate the Jews and anyone who testifies about Jesus and his Word.

"The earth helped the woman" speaks of the safe place that the Jewish people will find in the mountains. The Antichrist will not be able to get to their place of safety. The Jews who run to the mountains of safety will be out of the reach of the Antichrist.

Revelation 12:17 reads, "And the dragon was wroth with the woman, and went to make war with the remnant of her seed, which keep the commandments of God, and have the testimony of Jesus Christ."

The dragon will use the Antichrist and his government to wage war against the remnant of the Jews who did not escape and those among the Gentile population who give their lives to Jesus after the church has been raptured.

There are those who will say that none will be saved after the church is raptured, save those whose heads will be cut off for promoting the Word of God and testifying of Jesus. This is false doctrine and contrary to the Holy Bible. Such people also say that there will be no Holy Ghost around during this time because when the church is raptured, the Holy Spirit will go with it. *How wrong!* When the church is raptured, God will anoint 144,000 Jewish evangelists with a double portion of the Holy Ghost. They will witness to their Jewish brothers and sisters, and a great company of Jews will be saved (Revelation 15:2–4). Those whose heads are cut off for the Word of God are not Jews. They are Gentile believers. Remember, the Jews will be in the mountains that God has provided for them, a place of safety where the Antichrist cannot reach them. Do you not think that if God can save Jews during the time of the Gentiles' dispensation, he can save Gentiles during the time of the Jews' dispensation? Certainly, yes, yes, yes! There are those who referred to Second Thessalonians 2:10–12 reads, "And with all deceivableness of righteousness in them that perish; because they received not the love of the truth, that they might be saved. And for this cause God shall send them strong delusion, that they should believe a lie: that they all might be damned who believed not the truth, but had pleasure in unrighteousness."

Upon whom will God send a strong delusion? Those who do not love the truth and who take pleasure in unrighteousness, but not those who never heard the Word, nor those who heard but did not understand the Word. God will have mercy on whom he will. Many Gentiles will be saved after the church is raptured. But the Holy Ghost will still be present to convict the world of sin and unrighteousness, with judgment to come.

In fact, the Holy Ghost will be present in a greater measure, for wherever there is sin, grace is present to a much greater degree. God will not hand the world over to the devil. The earth and the fullness thereof is the Lord's. The Holy Ghost will reap a mighty harvest of Jews after the church is gone, and their heads will not be cut off!

Revelation 15:2–3 reads, "And I saw as it were a sea of glass mingled with fire: and them that had gotten the victory over the beast, and over his image, and over his mark, and over the number of his name, stand on the sea of glass, having the harps of God. And they sing the song of Moses the servant of God, and the song of the Lamb, saying, Great and marvellous are thy works, Lord God Almighty; just and true are thy ways, thou King of saints."

This group of saints represents the harvest of Jews who will be saved as a result of the preaching of the 144,000 Jewish evangelists. They will sing in heaven the songs of Moses and the Lamb. The Holy Ghost chose Moses so we would know that this group is strictly Jewish. The group in Revelation 20:4 whose heads are cut off are the Gentile group who will be saved after the church is raptured. Even they must come to God through the Holy Spirit. *For no person can come to God but by the Holy Spirit.*

The 144,000 Jews will be sealed with the Holy Ghost to carry on their evangelistic mission after the church is raptured. And they will be sealed with a double portion! So, will the Holy Spirit be present after the church is gone? A mighty yes! And in a greater measure! As a teacher, I can hold out my belt or any tool of correction. When the children see it, they are restrained, but when I move my belt or corrective device, they are not restrained.

He who letteth will let, until he be taken out of the way. The Holy Spirit is the restraining power that prevents the Antichrist from taking charge. When the Holy Spirit chooses to remove his restraint, the Antichrist will come. The Holy Spirit can move his restraint and still be present just as I can move the belt or other corrective measure and still be present. Let's not put God in our theological box and believe that God has to move himself completely out of the scene and give the earth over to the devil and his evil forces for the Antichrist to take up his position. This doctrine is completely wrong. I have been hearing this since I was a child, and I have never—and will never—swallow that pill. The Holy Spirit will be most present and active on earth in the lives of the 144,000 Jews, harvesting Jewish souls and also leading many Gentiles to Christ.

REVELATION CHAPTER 13

In Revelation 13:1, we read, "And I stood upon the sand of the sea, and saw a beast rise up out of the sea, having seven heads and ten horns, and upon his horns ten crowns, and upon his heads the name of blasphemy."

John is standing at a vantage point of observation and sees a beast rise up out of the sea. This beast is the Antichrist. It is the second time he is seen in a significant way rising in world politics. The first time is when he comes into power when the Lamb of God breaks the first seal at the beginning of the Antichrist's seven-year reign. This second time is when the first three and a half years of his reign have expired and he takes up a transformed manner of being autocratic as concerns human existence. He is supported by a ten-horned or a ten-toed kingdom with ten world leaders who will be in charge of specific demographic dominions and who will submit to him and give their allegiance to him. This is seen in Daniel chapters 2 and 7. Daniel 7:20–21 reads, "And of the ten horns that were in his head, and of the other which came up, and before whom three fell; even of that horn that had eyes, and a mouth that spake very great things, whose look was more stout than his fellows. I beheld, and the same horn made war with the saints, and prevailed against them." This horn is the selfsame Antichrist. And upon his head is the name of blasphemy. His kingdom will be in total opposition to God's and all that God stands for. That which is right will be made wrong and that which is wrong will be made right. For example, refusing to marry a gay couple will be met with a jail sentence and stiff fines. The Antichrist is called "the lawless one" in the scriptures.

Revelation 13:2 reads, "And the beast which I saw was like unto a leopard, and his feet were as the feet of a bear, and his mouth as the mouth of a lion: and the dragon gave him his power, and his seat, and great authority." That the beast is described as being like a leopard speaks to the fact that he will not be of a pure race. The leopard has white and black spots. The Antichrist will be of mixed origin, White and Black in nature. His feet are that of a bear. This speaks of his political strength. His mouth is the mouth of a lion. This speaks of his military might; the devil gave him his power. The devil has finally found a man whose heart is knitted together in one theme to oppose God. So the fallen dragon, the defeated one who has lost his place in the heavens, is seeking for a place among the sons of men to continue his diabolic moves against God.

The devil gives to the Antichrist his power of influence, and his seat, and his leadership abilities, and great authority with his supernatural abilities. Revelation 13:3 reads, "And I saw one of his heads as it were wounded to death; and his deadly wound was healed: and all the world wondered after the beast."

We read in Revelation 13:4, "And they worshipped the dragon which gave power unto the beast: and they worshipped the beast, saying, Who is like unto the beast? who is able to make war with him?" The devil has found his man of business who will be worshipped as the world recognizes from where he gets those powers. The world will unmistakably understand his rise to supreme power and his blasphemous statements against God. This reaffirms that his powers are demonic. The world will be unaware of the war that took place in the heavens that dethroned and humiliated the devil and his evil demons. They will be unaware that the presence of the devil on earth as a result of his having lost the battle in the heavens. They will be unaware that they are giving their worship and allegiance to the master of deceit, who has been routed and dethroned from his place in the heavens. The world will also worship the beast, saying, "Who is like unto the beast?" He will be one of a kind. We will come back to this idea when we discuss Revelation 13:12.

Revelation 13:5 reads, "And there was given unto him a mouth speaking great things and blasphemies; and power was given unto him to continue forty and two months." After the church is gone (raptured), the world will be in a catastrophic mess. The Antichrist will lose his life but will be restored to life again, but not by God's power. The seven-year period of his reign is distinctly divided into two parts: the first three-and-a-half-year period and the second three-and-a-half-year period.

Daniel 7:25 reads, "And he shall speak great words against the most High, and shall wear out the saints of the most High, and think to change times and laws: and they shall be given into his hand until a time and times and the dividing of time."

$$\text{Time} = 1 \text{ year} \times 2 \text{ years} \div 0.5 \text{ year} = 3.5 \text{ years.}$$

Revelation 13:6 reads, "And he opened his mouth in blasphemy against God, to blaspheme his name, and his tabernacle, and them that dwell in heaven." The Antichrist opposes all that is of God in heaven and on earth. There is something unique about the Antichrist when he is restored to life. There is a feeling of demonic pomposity about him that will arise in the second half of his reign.

Revelation 13:7 reads, "And it was given unto him to make war with the saints, and to overcome them: and power was given him over all kindreds, and tongues, and nations." Daniel 7:21 speaks of the Antichrist persecuting the saints of God. This relates to his persecuting the saints in the first half of his reign, the first three and a half years. But verse 25 speaks of him persecuting the saints for the latter three-and-a-half-year period—persecuting the people of God after the church is raptured for the last three and a half years.

Revelation 13:8 reads, "And all that dwell upon the earth shall worship him, whose names are not written in the book of life of the Lamb slain from the foundation of the world."

The Word of God does not say that all who dwell on the earth shall worship him. No, no, no! But the Word of God does say that all who dwell on the earth *whose names are not written in the book of life* shall worship him! So there will be Christians who will refuse to worship him. They would rather have their heads cut off or lose their lives than receive his mark or worship him. Praise the Lord! It's only the blood of Jesus that shields and will shield them from him. They will overcome the Antichrist by the blood of the Lamb and by the word of their testimony.

Revelation 13:9 reads, "If any man have an ear, let him hear." Sometimes profound statements of truth are made. People hear something profound and don't take hold of it, which results in eternal consequences of remorse. The Holy Spirit is saying to leave your old ways and harmonize with the gospel of Jesus Christ. You are either on God's side or on the devil's side. You are a worshipper of either God or Satan. You are either saved under the blood of Jesus or lost in sin. You are either righteous or unrighteous. You are either holy or unholy. You are either on your way to heaven or on your way to hell. The choice is yours. Choose ye this day whom ye will serve. For no person can serve both God and mammon. You have to love one and hate the other. Take heed of your life!

Revelation 13:10 reads, "He that leadeth into captivity shall go into captivity: he that killeth with the sword must be killed with the sword. Here is the patience and the faith of the saints."

When Jesus returns at the battle of Armageddon, after dealing with the armies that come up against him, he will send forth his armies to purge the land of all unwanted persons. Those who would be responsible for causing and capturing and imprisoning the saints of God, and who are alive at that time, will be given just judgment. They will be placed into captivity for life during the thousand-year reign of Christ. Those who killed Christians during the reign of the Antichrist and are alive when Jesus returns will be killed. They will not experience the blessed thousand-year reign of Christ. It will take forty-five days to purge the land before the thousand-year reign of Christ is brought into force.

Daniel 12:11–12 reads, "And from the time that the daily sacrifice shall be taken away, and the abomination that maketh desolate set up, *there shall be a thousand two hundred and ninety days*. Blessed is he that waiteth, and cometh to the *thousand three hundred and five and thirty days*" (emphasis added). Those Jews who flee to the mountains of Israel for safety during the second half of the three and a half years will be instructed to wait in their hiding places until cleanup operations are over. They will get the news that Jesus and his armies have defeated the Antichrist and his armies. Rejoicing will begin in their camps, but they will have to stay indoors until God and his armies do a general purging of the earth, which will last forty-five days. Jude 1:14–15 reads, "And Enoch also, the seventh from Adam, prophesied of these, saying, Behold, the Lord cometh with ten thousands of his saints, to execute judgment upon all, and to convince all that are ungodly among them of all their ungodly deeds which they have ungodly committed, and of all their hard speeches which ungodly sinners have spoken against him." The supernatural army seen in Joel chapter 2 are the saints who come with Christ on white horses.

After the battle has been won at Armageddon, the armies of the Lord will move to other places, beyond the walls of China to the mansions of Hollywood, to the deserts of Arabia, and all across this planet, till every knee bows and every tongue confesses that Jesus Christ is Lord to the glory of God the Father. Joel also sees the same army. Joel 2:1–11 reads as follows:

> Blow ye the trumpet in Zion, and sound an alarm in my holy mountain: let all the inhabitants of the land tremble: for the day of the Lord cometh, for it is nigh at hand; a day of darkness and of gloominess, a day of clouds and of thick darkness, as the morning spread upon the mountains: a great people and a strong; there hath not been ever the like, neither shall be any more after it, even to the years of many generations. A fire devoureth before them; and behind them a flame burneth: the land is as the garden of Eden before them, and behind them a desolate wilderness; yea, and nothing shall escape them. The appearance of them is as the appearance of horses; and as horsemen, so shall they run. Like the noise of chariots on the tops of mountains shall they leap, like the noise of a flame of fire that devoureth the stubble, as a strong people set in battle array. Before their face the people shall be much

pained: all faces shall gather blackness. They shall run like mighty men; they shall climb the wall like men of war; and they shall march everyone on his ways, and they shall not break their ranks: Neither shall one thrust another; they shall walk everyone in his path: and when they fall upon the sword, they shall not be wounded. They shall run to and fro in the city; they shall run upon the wall, they shall climb up upon the houses; they shall enter in at the windows like a thief. The earth shall quake before them; the heavens shall tremble: the sun and the moon shall be dark, and the stars shall withdraw their shining: And the Lord shall utter his voice before his army: for his camp is very great: for he is strong that executeth his word: for the day of the Lord is great and very terrible; and who can abide it?

"Here is the patience and the faith of the saints." The saints, when persecuted, will not take up arms to fight back. Knowing that the day of the vengeance of the Lord is coming, they will be part of the glorious army of the Lord to execute vengeance on the wicked.

Revelation 13:11–12 reads, "And I beheld another beast coming up out of the earth; and he had two horns like a lamb, and he spake as a dragon. And he exerciseth all the power of the first beast before him, and causeth the earth and them which dwell therein to worship the first beast, whose deadly wound was healed."

This second beast is the false prophet who will be working alongside the Antichrist. Down through the centuries, good people of God have mistakenly seen Revelation 17:5 as the Antichrist coming from Rome. But Revelation 13:11 clarifies Revelation 17:5. Revelation 17:5 speaks of an earthly system *coming from the earth*. Revelation 13:11 identifies the one *coming up out of the earth*, saying it will have two horns like a lamb. This is the false prophet. In other words, Revelation 17:5 and Revelation 13:11 are both speaking of the same individual—not the Antichrist, but the false prophet. Again I say that Revelation 13:11 brings clarity to Revelation 17:5. Rome will produce not the Antichrist but the final false prophet! The Roman Catholic Church is a religious organization, so this is what it will do. The Antichrist, on the other hand, as mentioned in Revelation 13:1, is seen coming from the sea.

It's a sea of people. The nations of this world will vote him into power. He will be the political genius of all time who will temporarily solve some of the world's problems. But when people are content enough to say that peace and safety now reign, sudden destruction shall come upon them.

The false prophet will persuade the world to worship the beast. The two great entities governing humankind at that time will be world politics headed by the Antichrist, along with a one world religious system headed by the false prophet.

We read in Revelation 13:13-14, "And he doeth great wonders, so that he maketh fire come down from heaven on the earth in the sight of men, and deceiveth them that dwell on the earth by the means of those miracles which he had power to do in the sight of the beast; saying to them that dwell on the earth, that they should make an image to the beast, which had the wound by a sword, and did live."

Second Thessalonians 2:8-10 reads, "And then shall that wicked one be revealed, whom the Lord shall consume with the spirit of his mouth, and shall destroy with the brightness of his coming: Even him, whose coming is after the working of Satan with all power and signs and lying wonders, and with all deceivableness of unrighteousness in them that perish; because they received not the love of the truth, that they might be saved."

We read in Revelation 13:15, "And he had power to give life unto the image of the beast, that the image of the beast should both speak, and cause that as many as would not worship the image of the beast should be killed." After the church is raptured, millions of millions of people will be missing, including the heads of various companies, leaders and workers of great enterprises, tradesmen, women, children, and babies. The world will do a census to determine the number of people on Planet Earth. This information shall be placed into a database. After this is done, a shocking compulsory program will be implemented -"the mark of the beast."

We read in Revelation 13:16–17, "And he causeth all, both small and great, rich and poor, free and bond, to receive a mark in their right hand, or in their foreheads: and that no man might buy or sell, save he that had the mark, or the name of the beast, or the number of his name."

When will this be done? At the second half of the seven-year period, which will be the latter three-and-a-half-year period. We have stated previously that in the first half of the seven-year reign of the Antichrist that money will still be used. Example: when the third horse rider comes forth, a voice proclaims, "A measure of wheat for *a penny*, and three measures of bailey for *a penny*" (emphasis added)

It is in the second half, after the church is gone, when the 666 mark will be implemented according to the scriptures.

Indeed, the system and the technology will be put in place beforehand, before the mark is implemented. For example, Revelation chapter 11 speaks of the two prophets who will be killed after they complete their testimony. And the whole world will see their dead bodies. This will be done via satellite system. The technology presently exists, but the event is still to come. In a similar way, the information for the chit system will be gathered beforehand, then the system will be implemented as a compulsory mark under the Antichrist's rule after the church is caught up and taken away.

The world will be brought under one system led by political and religious leaders. The economy will be under their rule and stewardship. The mark of the beast will be placed either on the right hand or in the center of forehead. It will be either (1) a mark, or (2) the name of the beast, or (3) the number of his name.

Revelation 13:18 reads, "Here is wisdom. Let him that hath understanding count the number of the beast: for it is the number of a man; and his number is six hundred threescore and six." The scripture admonishes us to have wisdom in calculating the number. In other words, it will not come out in boldface. You need to use some tact.

I would like to leave some clues with you:

- From the first of January to the day of the Antichrist's birth is 216 days, and 216 is actually 6 × 6 × 6.
- Giving each letter in his name the numerical value of 1 will add up to 18, which is actually 6 + 6 + 6.
- Placing a numerical value on his first name by using the alphabetical chart, for example, A as 1, B as 2, you get 36. When you add the numbers from 1 to 36, you will get 666.

So, you see, whether you stew him, fry him, or bake him, you will get 666! Wow! His first name also has a significant meaning, which I will not go into. I will leave that for you to do as homework. I will not give you everything on a platter. My aim is not to ridicule anyone but to give you the God-given facts of truth and reality.

REVELATION CHAPTER 14

We read in Revelation 14:1, "And I looked, and, lo, a Lamb stood on the mount Sion, and with him an hundred forty and four thousand, having his Father's name written in their foreheads." These Jews are saved by the sacrificial blood of the Lamb of God and have experienced the redemptive plan of God for their lives.

Verse 2 reads, "And I heard a voice from heaven, as the voice of many waters, and as the voice of a great thunder: and I heard the voice of harpers harping with their harps." The voice that John hears may be the voice of Almighty God welcoming them home. They have faithfully completed their evangelistic ministry and have won many Jews to Christ. They will be singing before the Lord.

Verse 3 reads, "And they sung as it were a new song before the throne, and before the four beasts, and the elders: and no man could learn that song but the hundred and forty and four thousand, which were redeemed from the earth." Their position is before the throne of God. They will sing and play musical instruments before the presence of God forever and ever.

They will form part of the Sanhedrin council, which will assist the elders in their divine role of leadership around the throne. The name of God will be on their foreheads.

We read in Revelation 14:4, "These are they which were not defiled with women; for they are virgins. These are they which follow the Lamb whithersoever he goeth. These were redeemed from among men, being the first-fruits unto God and to the Lamb." God reaps his harvest of Jewish souls and continues to reap through their preaching.

Revelation 14:5 reads, "And in their mouth was found no guile: for they are without fault before the throne of God."

Revelation 14:6–7 reads, "And I saw another angel fly in the midst of heaven, having the everlasting gospel to preach unto them that dwell on the earth, and to every nation, and kindred, and tongue, and people, saying with a loud voice, Fear God, and give glory to him; for the hour of his judgment is come: and worship him that made heaven, and earth, and the sea, and the fountains of waters." After the 144,000 Jews are raptured, God will use angels to preach the gospel. Things at this point will be too dangerous for any mortal person to preach the gospel without the aid of the angelic hosts.

Revelation 14:8 reads, "And there followed another angel, saying, Babylon is fallen, is fallen, that great city, because she made all nations drink of the wine of the wrath of her fornication." Many times we see ungodly people making ungodly laws, rules, and regulations set up by those in authority who do not see the sinister plan of the devil working behind the scenes. That's why we need to pray for our leaders, so that we will be able to live a quiet and peaceable life. These laws have corrupted the entire world.

Revelation 14:9–11 reads as follows:

> And the third angel followed them, saying with a loud voice, If any man worship the beast and his

image, and receive his mark in his forehead, or in his hand, The same shall drink of the wine of the wrath of God, which is poured out without mixture into the cup of his indignation; and he shall be tormented with fire and brimstone in the presence of the holy angels, and in the presence of the Lamb: And the smoke of their torment ascendeth up for ever and ever: and they have no rest day nor night, who worship the beast and his image, and whosoever receiveth the mark of his name.

Men and women who receive the mark of the beast will be forewarned that this act will be punishable by God to the highest degree with torture and eternal damnation.

Revelation 14:12 reads, "Here is the patience of the saints: here are they that keep the commandments of God, and the faith of Jesus." God is not talking about the Ten Commandments here but of those who have accepted his love, mercy, and grace and who walk in his precepts and in the light of his Word. They will love not their lives to the death.

Revelation 14:13 reads, "And I heard a voice from heaven saying unto me, Write, Blessed are the dead which die in the Lord from henceforth: Yea, saith the Spirit, that they may rest from their labours; and their works do follow them." This scripture is proof that people will be saved in perilous times like those even after the church is raptured. Their works will follow them. They will be rewarded for what they do for Christ. All that they do for Christ will last for all eternity. The good Lord will reward them with eternal treasures (Revelation 20:4).

Revelation 14:14–20 reads as follows:

> And I looked, and behold a white cloud, and upon the cloud one sat like unto the Son of man, having on his head a golden crown, and in his hand a sharp sickle. And another angel came out of the temple, crying

with a loud voice to him that sat on the cloud, Thrust in thy sickle, and reap: for the time is come for thee to reap; for the harvest of the earth is ripe. And he that sat on the cloud thrust in his sickle on the earth; and the earth was reaped. And another angel came out of the temple which is in heaven, he also having a sharp sickle. And another angel came out from the altar, which had power over fire; and cried with a loud cry to him that had the sharp sickle, saying, Thrust in thy sharp sickle, and gather the clusters of the vine of the earth; for her grapes are fully ripe. And the angel thrust in his sickle into the earth, and gathered the vine of the earth, and cast it into the great winepress of the wrath of God. And the winepress was trodden without the city, and blood came out of the winepress, even unto the horse bridles, by the space of a thousand and six hundred furlongs.

The Son of man, Jesus, is the reaper, and he will be ably assisted by the angels of God. The wheat, he will gather into his barn, but the chaff, he will burn with unquenchable fire.

REVELATION CHAPTER 15

In Revelation 15:1, we read, "And I saw another sign in heaven, great and marvellous, seven angels having the seven last plagues; for in them is filled up the wrath of God." God will use the Lamb of God to break the seven seals. God will then use seven trumpet angels to execute seven trumpet judgments. And now he is about to use seven angels with seven vials filled with the wrath of God to execute his wrath. God is well organized in dealing with and executing his plan of redemption and judgment. Let's not take him for granted.

Revelation 15:2-3 reads, "And I saw as it were a sea of glass mingled with fire: and them that had gotten the victory over the beast, and over his image, and over his mark, and over the number of his name, stand on the sea of glass, having the harps of God. And they sing the song of Moses the servant of God, and the song of the Lamb, saying, Great and marvelous are thy works, Lord God Almighty; just and true are thy ways, thou King of saints." This group of saints will gain victory over the following:

- the beast
- his image
- his mark
- the number of his name. (They have to be living during this period.)

This group of believers is made up strictly of Jews who have been saved as a result of the preaching of the 144,000 Jewish evangelists. The Holy Ghost included "singing the songs of Moses and the Lamb" so as to identify this group as Jews who can trace their ancestral lineage to that of Abraham, Isaac, and Jacob. They are standing on the sea of glass. This figurative language simply means a vast area reserved before the throne of God specially designed for this group of saints. They have harps in their hands and are singing, which simply means that they are musicians. This sea of glass is the same area mentioned in Revelation 4:6. The gold in that area is so pure that it looks like glass. These Jewish worshippers will be energized by the fire of the Holy Ghost to sing the glorious songs of praise to God throughout the countless ages of eternity. That's their eternal position. O the massive plan of God is being unfolded!

Revelation 15:4 reads, "Who shall not fear thee, O Lord, and glorify thy name? for thou only art holy: for all nations shall come and worship before thee; for thy judgments are made manifest." This group has to be living when the judgments of God are poured out on earth, but the church will not be around at that time.

We find the following in Revelation 15:5-8:

And after that I looked, and, behold, the temple of the tabernacle of the testimony in heaven was opened: And the seven angels came out of the temple, having the seven plagues, clothed in pure and white linen, and having their breasts girded with golden girdles. And one of the four beasts gave unto the seven angels seven golden vials full of the wrath of God, who liveth for ever and ever. And the temple was filled with smoke from the glory of God, and from his power; and no man was able to enter into the temple, till the seven plagues of the seven angels were fulfilled.

Thanks be to God for storing up wrath to be released at a particular time. Some people sin without regard for God. It looks like God doesn't care about what we do on earth or how we live. But we will be proven to be very wrong about that. God does care, and he will pour out the fierceness of his wrath upon unrepentant humankind. Again he will use specially assigned angels for the task. The four beasts that are before the throne will sanction the outpouring of the wrath of God. One of them will give to the seven angels seven golden vials filled with the wrath of God, who liveth forever and ever. God is a holy God, and he demands holiness, without which no person shall see the Lord.

REVELATION CHAPTER 16

And I heard a great voice out of the temple saying to the seven angels, Go your ways, and pour out the vials of the wrath of God upon the earth. And the first went, and poured out his vial upon the earth; and there fell a noisome and grievous sore upon the men which had the mark of the beast, and upon them which worshipped his image. And the second angel poured out his vial upon the sea; and it became as the blood of a dead man: and every living soul died in the sea. And the third angel poured out his vial upon the rivers and fountains of waters; and they became blood. And I heard the angel of the waters say, Thou art righteous, O Lord, which art, and wast, and shalt be, because thou hast judged thus. For they have shed the blood of saints and prophets, and thou hast given them blood to drink; for they are worthy. And I heard another out of the altar say, Even so, Lord God Almighty, true and righteous are thy judgments. And the fourth angel poured out his vial upon the sun; and power was given unto him to scorch men with fire. And men were scorched with great heat, and blasphemed the name of God, which hath power over these plagues: and they repented not to give him glory. And the fifth angel poured out his vial upon the seat of the beast; and his kingdom was full of darkness; and they gnawed their tongues for pain, and blasphemed the God of heaven because of their pains and their sores, and repented not of their deeds. And the sixth angel poured out his vial upon the great river Euphrates; and the water thereof was dried up, that the way of the kings of the east might be prepared. And I saw three unclean spirits like frogs come out of the mouth of the dragon, and out of the mouth of the beast, and out of the mouth of the false prophet. For they are the spirits of devils, working miracles, which go forth unto the kings of the earth and of the whole world, to gather them to the battle of that great day of God Almighty. Behold, I come as a thief. Blessed is he that watcheth, and keepeth his garments, lest he walk naked, and they see his shame. And he gathered them together into a place called in the Hebrew tongue Armageddon. And the seventh angel poured out his vial into the air; and there came a great voice out of the temple of heaven, from the throne, saying, It is done. And there were voices, and thunders, and lightnings; and there was a great earthquake, such as was not since men were upon the earth, so mighty an earthquake, and so great. And the great city was divided into three parts, and the cities of the nations fell: and great Babylon came in remembrance before God, to give unto her the cup of the wine of the fierceness of his wrath. And every island fled away, and the mountains were not found. And there fell upon men a great hail out of heaven, every stone about the weight of a talent: and men blasphemed God because of the plague of the hail; for the plague thereof was exceeding great.

Revelation chapter 16 deals with the wrath of God being poured out upon the earth. There will never be another time like this on Planet Earth. In Matthew 24:21 Jesus said, "For then shall be great tribulation, such as was not since the beginning of the world to this time, no, nor ever shall be." This is talking about the devastating effects of the pouring out of each vial, mentioned above. Jesus is certainly coming back, not as a babe in a manger this time, but as King of kings and Lord of lords. He will come amid the clouds of heaven with power and great glory and authority. He will reign over the House of David, and to his kingdom there shall be no end. May we surrender our lives to Jesus before it is too late! God is offering us royal robes of righteousness. Second Corinthians 5:21 says, "For he hath made him to be sin for us, *who knew no sin*; that we might be made the righteousness of God in him" (emphasis added).

When the seventh angel pours out his vial into the air, there comes a great voice out of the temple of heaven, from the throne, saying, "It is done."

God is an orderly God who does things after the counsel of his own will. The Prince of the Power of the Air (the devil) finally will be judged. His demonic linkage and communication network will both be shattered. He will be rousted not only from the heavens above but also from the air. What a defeated foe! The mystery of iniquity will be given a devastating blow that never will be recoverable from. The great voice of God Almighty from his throne will back up the action of the seventh angel. He will fortify and consolidate the victory by saying, "It is done!"

When that is done, there will be voices, thunder and lightning, and a great earthquake such as has not been seen since humankind appeared upon the earth, so mighty and so great. Then the great city will be divided into three parts, and the cities of the nation will fall. Great Babylon will come in remembrance before God to be given the cup of the wine of the fierceness of his wrath.

Isaiah 24:18–23 reads as follows:

> And it shall come to pass, that he who fleeth from the noise of the fear shall fall into the pit; and he that cometh up out of the midst of the pit shall be taken in the snare: for the windows from on high are open, and the foundations of the earth do shake. The earth is utterly broken down, the earth is clean dissolved, the earth is moved exceedingly. The earth shall reel to and fro like a drunkard, and shall be removed like a cottage; and the transgression thereof shall be heavy upon it; and it shall fall, and not rise again. And it shall come to pass in that day, that the Lord shall punish the host of the high ones that are on high, and the kings of the earth upon the earth. And they shall be gathered together, as prisoners are gathered in the pit, and shall be shut up in the prison, and after many days shall they be visited. Then the moon shall be confounded, and the sun ashamed, when the Lord of hosts shall reign in mount Zion, and in Jerusalem, and before his ancients gloriously.

REVELATION CHAPTER 17

And there came one of the seven angels which had the seven vials, and talked with me, saying unto me, Come hither; I will shew unto thee the judgment of the great harlot that sitteth upon many waters: With whom the kings of the earth have committed fornication, and the inhabitants of the earth have been made drunk with the wine of her fornication. So he carried me away in the spirit into the wilderness: and I saw a woman sit upon a scarlet colored beast, full of names of blasphemy, having seven heads and ten horns. And the woman was arrayed in purple and scarlet color, and decked with gold and precious stones and pearls, having a golden cup in her hand full of abominations and filthiness of her fornication: And upon her forehead was a name written, MYSTERY, BABYLON THE GREAT, THE MOTHER OF HARLOTS AND ABOMINATIONS OF THE EARTH. And I saw the woman drunken with the blood of the saints, and with the blood of the martyrs of Jesus: and when I saw her, I wondered with great admiration. And the angel said unto me, Wherefore didst thou marvel? I will tell thee the mystery of the woman, and of the beast that carrieth her, which hath the seven heads and ten horns. The beast that thou sawest was, and is not; and shall ascend out of the bottomless pit, and go into perdition: and they that dwell on the earth shall wonder, whose names were not written in the book of life from the foundation of the world, when they behold the beast that was, and is not, and yet is. And here is the mind which hath wisdom. The seven heads are seven mountains, on which the woman sitteth. And there are seven kings: five are fallen, and one is, and the other is not yet come; and when he cometh, he must continue a short space. And the beast that was, and is not, even he is the eighth, and is of the seven, and goeth into perdition. And the ten horns which thou sawest are ten kings, which have received no kingdom as yet; but receive power as kings one hour with the beast. These have one mind, and shall give their power and strength unto the beast. These shall make war with the Lamb, and the Lamb shall overcome them: for he is Lord of lords, and King of kings: and they that are with him are called, and chosen, and faithful. And he saith unto me, The waters which thou sawest, where the harlot sitteth, are peoples, and multitudes, and nations, and tongues. And the ten horns which thou sawest upon the beast, these shall hate the harlot, and shall make her desolate and naked, and shall eat her flesh, and burn her with fire. For God hath put in their hearts to fulfill his will, and to agree, and give their kingdom unto the beast, until the words of God shall be fulfilled. And the woman which thou sawest is that great city, which reigneth over the kings of the earth.

God is going to judge this evil, corrupt, wicked, and ungodly system, which is being personified here in as a great harlot. The unseen spiritual powers of darkness pervade the norms, laws, morals, and spiritual values of our societies. Human beings are lovers of pleasures more than lovers of God. First Timothy 4:1-3 states, "Now the Spirit speaketh expressly, that in the latter times some shall depart from the faith, giving heed to seducing spirits, and doctrines of devils; speaking lies in hypocrisy; having their conscience seared with a hot iron; forbidding to marry, and commanding to abstain from meats, which God hath created to be received with thanksgiving of them which believe and know the truth." Second Timothy 3:1-5 states,

"This know also, that in the last days perilous times shall come. For men shall be lovers of their own selves, covetous, boasters, proud, blasphemers, disobedient to parents, unthankful, unholy, without natural affection, trucebreakers, false accusers, incontinent, fierce, despisers of those that are good, traitors, heady, high-minded, lovers of pleasures more than lovers of God; having a form of godliness, but denying the power thereof: from such turn away."

The great harlot sits on many waters. She has allowed her ungodly influence to permeate the nations of the earth. The kings of the earth and the leaders of nations have walked hand in hand with her philosophies and have promoted her ideologies. John was carried away in the spirit into the wilderness to see the sinister master operative plan of the devil. You will notice as you go deeper into this chapter that the woman and the beast both have seven heads and ten horns. The woman represents the religious aspect of the ungodly system; wherever the woman is, you will find the beast. The beast ascends from the bottomless pit. In his death he goes there, but he ascends when he is brought back to life to continue his reign for the further three and a half years to complete the seven-year period.

So much is said by theologians concerning verses 10–11 of Revelation chapter 17. One thing I do know is that a former head of state will be coming back to serve as the head of the New World Order.

With reference to verse 10, the ten-toed kingdom in the book of Daniel is equivalent to the ten horns in the book of Revelation. The leaders of the world will walk in harmony with the Antichrist to fulfill his objectives, ultimately unwittingly fulfilling God's divine purpose. Verse 14 shows that the ultimate showdown in this war will happen at the battle of Armageddon. Those accompanying Jesus at the forefront to this battle are chosen warriors of the faith.

Revelation 17:15 says, "And he saith unto me, The waters which thou sawest, where the harlot sitteth, are peoples, and multitudes, and nations, and tongues." This verse serves as a helpful tool in understanding some figurative language in the book of Revelation. Verses 16 and 17 show that God shall bring judgment upon Mystery

Babylon. He can use anyone or any group of kings to accomplish his divine purpose. Verse 18 shows that it is from the headquarters of the United Nations that the Antichrist will reign and rule Planet Earth.

REVELATION CHAPTER 18

Chapter 17 of Revelation deals with the religious aspect of Mystery Babylon, whereas chapter 18 deals with the political aspect of Mystery Babylon.

God is going to judge the great harlot who corrupted the earth for her great sins and atrocities against God and his saints. She and the nations that have been partakers of her godless systems will experience the full wrath of God.

John heard another voice from heaven, this one saying, "Come out of her, my people, that ye be not partakers of her sins, and that ye receive not of her plagues."

People will still be saved during this period of judgment. Again, God is going to judge this ungodly world. The kings, the merchants, the shipmasters, and all who partake in the world's pleasures shall experience God's judgment.

Obadiah 1:15 says, "For the day of the Lord is near upon all the heathen: as thou hast done, it shall be done unto thee: thy reward shall return upon thine own head." Jeremiah 17:18 says, "Let them be confounded that persecute me, but let not me be confounded: let them be dismayed, but let not me be dismayed: bring upon them the day of evil, and destroy them with double destruction."

The trading mark 666 will prove to be folly, and those who receive it will know that they have wrought folly on their own souls.

REVELATION CHAPTER 19

And after these things I heard a great voice of much people in heaven, saying, Alleluia; Salvation, and glory, and honor, and power, unto the Lord our God:

For true and righteous are his judgments: for he hath judged the great harlot, which did corrupt the earth with her fornication, and hath avenged the blood of his servants at her hand. And again they said, Alleluia. And her smoke rose up for ever and ever. And the four and twenty elders and the four beasts fell down and worshipped God that sat on the throne, saying, Amen; Alleluia. And a voice came out of the throne, saying, Praise our God, all ye his servants, and ye that fear him, both small and great. And I heard as it were the voice of a great multitude, and as the voice of many waters, and as the voice of mighty thunderings, saying, Alleluia: for the Lord God omnipotent reigneth. Let us be glad and rejoice, and give honor to him: for the marriage of the Lamb is come, and his wife hath made herself ready. And to her was granted that she should be arrayed in fine linen, clean and white: for the fine linen is the righteousness of saints. And he saith unto me, Write, Blessed are they which are called unto the marriage supper of the Lamb. And he saith unto me, These are the true sayings of God. And I fell at his feet to worship him. And he said unto me, See thou do it not: I am thy fellow servant, and of thy brethren that have the testimony of Jesus: worship God: for the testimony of Jesus is the spirit of prophecy. And I saw heaven opened, and behold a white horse; and he that sat upon him was called Faithful and True, and in righteousness he doth judge and make war. His eyes were as a flame of fire, and on his head were many crowns; and he had a name written, that no man knew, but he himself. And he was clothed with a vesture dipped in blood: and his name is called The Word of God. And the armies which were in heaven followed him upon white horses, clothed in fine linen, white and clean. And out of his mouth goeth a sharp sword, that with it he should smite the nations: and he shall rule them with a rod of iron: and he treadeth the winepress of the fierceness and wrath of Almighty God. And he hath on his vesture and on his thigh a name written, King of Kings, and Lord of Lords. And I saw an angel standing in the sun; and he cried with a loud voice, saying to all the fowls that fly in the midst of heaven, Come and gather yourselves together unto the supper of the great God; That ye may eat the flesh of kings, and the flesh of captains, and the flesh of mighty men, and the flesh of horses, and of them that sit on them, and the flesh of all men, both free and bond, both small and great. And I saw the beast, and the kings of the earth, and their armies, gathered together to make war against him that sat on the horse, and against his army. And the beast was taken, and with him the false prophet that wrought miracles before him, with which he deceived them that had received the mark of the beast, and them that worshipped his image. These both were cast alive into a lake of fire burning with brimstone. And the remnant were slain with the sword of him that sat upon the horse, which sword proceeded out of his mouth: and all the fowls were filled with their flesh.

A loud crescendo of praise will be heard in heaven. The saints of God will be in perfect harmony and of one accord giving praise to God for his wonderful works of salvation and for judging the great harlot who corrupted the earth, also for avenging the blood of his servants at her hand. All of heaven will be in agreement with, and in unison toward, God's action.

The countless multitude of saints mentioned in Revelation

7:9–10, together with all the other groups of resurrected saints, will join the twenty-four elders and the four beasts in giving praises to God Almighty, whose power is manifested in salvation and judgment. Divine consummation of the bridegroom and the bride is to take place before she comes to earth with him to reign for a thousand years. The bride is now called his *wife*. The love of God for the church is so real and true that the human marriage of a man and his wife will fade into the shadows when the true substance shines its light in marriage between Christ and his church.

After the church has been caught up, taken away, and given white robes, it still will have to go through the bema judgment of God for its rewards.

This bema judgment must take place before the marriage ceremony, so it is reasonable to believe that while God is judging the inhabitants of the earth for their evil deeds, he will be rewarding his saints for their good works. We must always remember that salvation is by grace, mercy, and love that comes from God, "not of works lest any man should boast" (Ephesians 2:4–8). Nevertheless, God's reward is with him to give to every person according to his or her works. First Corinthians 3:13–15 states, "Every man's work shall be made manifest: for the day shall declare it, because it shall be revealed by fire; and the fire shall try every man's work of what sort it is. If any man's work abide which he hath built thereupon, he shall receive a reward. If any man's work shall be burned, he shall suffer loss: but he himself shall be saved; yet so as by fire."

After the saints have passed through the fire, the same white robes now will be seen as fine linen, clean and white, for fine linen is the righteousness of the saints. Our God is a consuming fire! He is holy, holy, holy! Thanks be to God for the bride, who is called to the marriage supper of the Lamb. After this supper is completed, the relationship between Jesus and the bride will become a relationship between a husband and his wife. What an eternal privilege!

When God tells John to write and then affirms the statements to be true, you know it will come to pass without a shadow of doubt.

John saw all the marvelous revelations of God's great plan. He was so filled with gratitude that he fell at the feet of the angel who had shown him these things, to worship. But the angel warned him not to do so, saying worship belongs to God alone and that John must direct his worship to God. The testimony of Jesus is the Spirit of prophecy. Prophecy is both (1) foretelling and (2) telling forth.

Jesus's coming to earth will be a dreadful experience for the ungodly. Revelation 1:7 reads, "Behold, he cometh with clouds; and every eye shall see him, and they also which pierced him: and all kindreds of the earth shall wail because of him. Even so, amen." This warrior has all knowledge. He is omniscient. He has fought many battles through the ages gone and comes to fight this final battle. Our God is a man of war who uses all his past victorious experiences in this war. Humankind is really no match for God regardless of their suffocating number of weapons of war. These are like ashes below God's glorious feet. It's always heel versus head, the heel of the woman's seed crushing the head of the serpent (Genesis 3:15).

Generally, warriors of this earth do not want their blood to be shed. But this warrior comes with a vesture dipped in blood. It's the blood of the cross. It's the blood of redemption. He has the power to redeem not only humankind but also the earth. The devil, who once tempted Christ and offered him the kingdom of this world, now has to bow in awesome despair as the rightful Redeemer who repurchased the earth, its dominions and kingdoms, is now coming to redeem it. The forces of darkness will remember their humiliating defeat at the cross when they see him coming with his vesture dipped in blood. His name is called the Word of God. He is responsible for creating the universe. Hebrews 1:1–3 states, "God, who at sundry times and in divers manners spake in time past unto the fathers by the prophets, hath in these last days spoken unto us by his Son, whom he hath appointed heir of all things, by whom also he made the worlds; who being the brightness of his glory, and the express image of his person, and upholding all things by the word of his power, when he had by himself purged our sins, sat down on the right hand of the Majesty on high." John 1:10 states, "He was in the world, and the world was made by him, and the world knew him not." Colossians 1:14–17 states, "In whom we have redemption through his blood, even the forgiveness of sins: who is the image of the invisible God, the firstborn of every creature: For by him were all things created, that are in heaven, and that are in earth, visible and invisible, whether they be thrones, or dominions, or principalities, or powers: all things were created by him, and for him: And he is before all things, and by him all things consist." This army is the church of Jesus Christ. The same type of clothing is seen being worn by this army, namely, fine linen, clean and white. This is the wife of Christ coming to spend one thousand years on a honeymoon experience with him.

It's the same army predicted by Enoch in Jude 1:14–15. It's the same army in Joel 2:2, with an extension of their activities. The Lord will use the power of his Word to defeat and subdue the armies of the nations of the world that will come up against him. Indeed, Jesus Christ is King of kings and Lord of lords.

Those hungry birds will be so glad to have their bellies filled with the supper of the great God, who had little to eat before, because of the judgments that will be poured out at that time on the earth and sea. These birds will devour the carcasses of those soldiers who come up against Christ, and will eat with awesome delight.

Zechariah 14:12–15 reads as follows:

> And this shall be the plague wherewith the Lord will smite all the people that have fought against Jerusalem; their flesh shall consume away while they stand upon their feet, and their eyes shall consume away in their holes, and their tongue shall consume away in their mouth. And it shall come to pass in that day, that a great tumult from the Lord shall be among them; and they shall lay hold everyone on the hand of his neighbour, and his hand shall rise up against the hand of his neighbour. And Judah also shall fight at Jerusalem; and the wealth of all the heathen round about shall be gathered together,

gold, and silver, and apparel, in great abundance. And so shall be the plague of the horse, of the mule, of the camel, and of the ass, and of all the beasts that shall be in these tents, as this plague.

This is not the nuclear warheads of humankind that will be released. This is *God at war*—a higher device than the nuclear warfare of humankind. If it were nuclear warfare, then the eagles would not be able to survive, much less to eat the flesh of captains, mighty men of war, or the flesh of the free and bond, small and great. It would seem that in this war even the notorious criminals will be given retribution to fight against Christ.

This has also been predicted by Jesus in Matthew chapter 24, concerning his Second Coming. Matthew 24:26–28 reads, "Wherefore if they shall say unto you, Behold, he is in the desert; go not forth: behold, he is in the secret chambers; believe it not. For as the lightning cometh out of the east, and shineth even unto the west; so shall also the coming of the Son of man be. For wheresoever the carcase is, there will the eagles be gathered together." It is amazing to see that the first occupants of the lake of fire will be the Antichrist and the false prophet. They will not be killed in this battle. God will preserve them alive for instant judgment. They will be cast alive into the lake of fire that burns with brimstone. The devil will join them after the thousand-year reign of Christ with his saints.

Other Scriptures Supporting the Battle of Armageddon

Zephaniah 3:8: "Therefore wait ye upon me, saith the Lord, until the day that I rise up to the prey: for my determination is to gather the nations, that I may assemble the kingdoms, to pour upon them mine indignation, even all my fierce anger: for all the earth shall be devoured with the fire of my jealousy."

Isaiah 66:15–16: "For, behold, the Lord will come with fire, and with his chariots like a whirlwind, to render his anger with fury, and his rebuke with flames of fire. For by fire and by his sword will the Lord plead with all flesh: and the slain of the Lord shall be many."

Isaiah 13:13: "Therefore I will shake the heavens, and the earth shall remove out of her place, in the wrath of the Lord of hosts, and in the day of his fierce anger."

2 Thessalonians 2:8: "And then shall that Wicked be revealed, whom the Lord shall consume with the spirit of his mouth, and shall destroy with the brightness of his coming."

Joel 3:14–16: "Multitudes, multitudes in the valley of decision: for the day of the Lord is near in the valley of decision. The sun and the moon shall be darkened, and the stars shall withdraw their shining. The Lord also shall roar out of Zion, and utter his voice from Jerusalem; and the heavens and the earth shall shake: but the Lord will be the hope of his people, and the strength of the children of Israel."

REVELATION CHAPTER 20

And I saw an angel come down from heaven, having the key of the bottomless pit and a great chain in his hand. And he laid hold on the dragon, that old serpent, which is the Devil, and Satan, and bound him a thousand years, and cast him into the bottomless pit, and shut him up, and set a seal upon him, that he should deceive the nations no more, till the thousand years should be fulfilled: and after that he must be loosed a little season. And I saw thrones, and they sat upon them, and judgment was given unto them: and I saw the souls of them that were beheaded for the witness of Jesus, and for the word of God, and which had not worshipped the beast, neither his image, neither had received his mark upon their foreheads, or in their hands; and they lived and reigned with Christ a thousand years. But the rest of the dead lived not again until the thousand years were finished. This is the first resurrection. Blessed and holy is he that hath part in the first resurrection: on such the second death hath no power, but they shall be priests of God and of Christ, and shall reign with him a thousand years. And when the thousand years are expired, Satan shall be loosed out of his prison, and shall go out to deceive the nations which are in the four quarters of the earth, Gog and Magog, to gather them together to battle: the number of whom is as the sand of the sea. And they went up on the breadth of the earth, and compassed the camp of the saints about, and the beloved city: and fire came down from God out of heaven, and devoured them. And the devil that deceived them was cast into the lake of fire and brimstone, where the beast and the false prophet are, and shall be tormented day and night for ever and ever. it, from whose face the earth and the heaven fled away; and there was found no place for them. And I saw the dead, small and great, stand before God; and the books were opened: and another book was opened, which is the book of life: and the dead were judged out of those things which were written in the books, according to their works. And the sea gave up the dead which were in it; and death and hell delivered up the dead which were in them: and they were judged every man according to their works.

And death and hell were cast into the lake of fire.
This is the second death. And whosoever was not
found written in the book of life was cast into the
lake of fire.

It would seem that the defeat of the dragon when he lost his place
in the heavens (Revelation 12:7–12) was so humiliating that he was
stripped of many of his combative powers. Here it takes just one angel
to bind him up. The scripture does not say "I saw a *mighty angel* come
down from heaven," as in other scriptures; it simply says, "And I saw
an angel come down from heaven." What a defeated foe is he!

The bottomless pit and the lake of fire and brimstone are two
different places. The devil is the master of deception, so even in the
bottomless pit a seal had to be placed on him—even when he is all
chained up so that he will not be able to deceive the nations until the
thousand years are fulfilled.

I believe that not only will the devil be bound and cast into
the bottomless pit during that period but also all the fallen angels
with him.

Zechariah 13:1–2 states, "In that day there shall be a fountain
opened to the house of David and to the inhabitants of Jerusalem for
sin and for uncleanness. And it shall come to pass in that day, saith
the Lord of hosts, that I will cut off the names of the idols out of the
land, and they shall no more be remembered: and also *I will cause
the prophets and the unclean spirit to pass out of the land*" (emphasis
added).

Revelation 20:4 speaks of a resurrection of saints whose heads
are cut off for believing in the Word of God and testifying of Jesus.

It must be noted that this group is not a part of the bridal party.
They will be resurrected at the end of the battle of Armageddon.
They will have been around during the time of the compulsory
mark of the beast. The qualifying clause reading that they had not
worshipped the beast, "neither his image, neither had received his
mark upon their foreheads or in their hands," attests to this fact.
Carrying a Bible, testifying about Jesus, or spreading the message

of salvation will be a criminal offense punishable by death. These people are the Gentile group of Christians who will have been saved. Remember, the Jews were instructed to flee to the mountains, which will be their place of safety and where they will be nourished for the second three-and-a-half-year period.

In verse 5 we see that the rest of the dead will be resurrected at the end of the thousand-year reign of Christ to be judged. The term "this is the first resurrection" is easy to misunderstand. One may feel that it is the first-time saints who will be resurrected. But the term "first resurrection" indicates the resurrection of the righteous. Prior the thousand-year reign of Christ, the resurrection of the righteous is basically carried out in five parts. It's like an orange with many sections. First Corinthians 15:23-24 reads, "Every man in his own order" (order of the resurrection). The order is (1) Christ the first fruits Matthew 27:51-53, see also 1 Corinthians 15:20; (2) they that are Christ at his coming (rapture) 1 Thessalonians 4:14-18, 1 Corinthians 15:51-58; (3) The 144,000 Jews are flaming evangelist. Revelation chapter 7 and 14; (4) The Jewish remnant saved and standing on the sea of glass as a result of the preaching 144,000 Jews. Revelation 15:2-4; and (5) the Gentile group of martyrs who will be saved after the church is raptured. Verse 6 assures us that it's the redeemed who are holy and blessed. Ephesians 1:3 states, "Blessed be the God and Father of our Lord Jesus Christ, who hath blessed us with all spiritual blessings in heavenly places in Christ."

The second death will be a judgment sentence passed by God on the unrepentant sinners, who will be cast into the *everlasting flames of fire*. All those who are a part of the first resurrection will reign with Christ for one thousand years.

When the thousand years are expired, Satan shall be loosed out of his prison. God then has a final mission for the devil. The billions of people who will have been reproducing during the thousand years must be sifted. So the devil, when he is loosed, will influence and deceive great multitudes of people as the sand upon the sea to come up against Christ and his saints. God will release fire from heaven, and they will be consumed.

The devil will then be cast into the lake of fire, burning with brimstone, where the beast and the false prophet are. The present tense *are* is used to indicate that the beast and the false prophet are and will forever be in the lake of fire that burns with brimstone. They will be cast there at the beginning of the thousand-year reign of Christ. At the end of that period, they will remain alive there. Having survived one thousand years of torture, they will continue to be tortured for all eternity. The devil will now join them and will be tormented forever and ever. Amen. As we read in Revelation 20:10, "And the devil that deceived them was cast into the lake of fire and brimstone, where the beast and the false prophet are, and shall be tormented day and night for ever and ever."

One might like to ask the question, will anyone born during the thousand-year reign of Christ be saved? Let's turn to Psalm 72 for the answer. Remember, Psalm 72 deals with the thousand-year reign of Christ. Verses 8–16 read as follows:

> He shall have dominion also from sea to sea, and from the river unto the ends of the earth. They that dwell in the wilderness shall bow before him; and his enemies shall lick the dust. The kings of Tarshish and of the isles shall bring presents: the kings of Sheba and Seba shall offer gifts. Yea, all kings shall fall down before him: all nations shall serve him. For he shall deliver the needy when he crieth; the poor also, and him that hath no helper. He shall spare the poor and needy, and shall save the souls of the needy. He shall redeem their soul from deceit and violence: and precious shall their blood be in his sight. And he shall live, and to him shall be given of the gold of Sheba: prayer also shall be made for him continually; and daily shall he be praised. There shall be an handful of corn in the earth upon the top of the mountains; the fruit thereof shall shake

like Lebanon: and they of the city shall flourish like grass of the earth.

How will life be during the thousand-year reign of Christ? Isaiah 11:4–9 states:

> But with righteousness shall he judge the poor, and reprove with equity for the meek of the earth: and he shall smite the earth with the rod of his mouth, and with the breath of his lips shall he slay the wicked. And righteousness shall be the girdle of his loins, and faithfulness the girdle of his reins. The wolf also shall dwell with the lamb, and the leopard shall lie down with the kid; and the calf and the young lion and the fatling together; and a little child shall lead them. And the cow and the bear shall feed; their young ones shall lie down together: and the lion shall eat straw like the ox. And the sucking child shall play on the hole of the asp, and the weaned child shall put his hand on the cockatrice' den. They shall not hurt nor destroy in all my holy mountain: for the earth shall be full of the knowledge of the Lord, as the waters cover the sea.

Isaiah 9:6, 7 states, "For unto us a child is born, unto us a son is given: and the government shall be upon his shoulder: and his name shall be called Wonderful, Counsellor, the mighty God, the everlasting Father, the Prince of Peace. Of the increase of his government and peace there shall be no end, upon the throne of David, and upon his kingdom, to order it, and to establish it with judgment and with justice from henceforth even forever. The zeal of the Lord of hosts will perform this."

It will be awesome, frightening reality when the Savior becomes the judge. I believe that this judgment will take place on earth. Every living soul who has not been resurrected in the first resurrection will be resurrected then, judged by God, and then cast into the lake of fire, where they will be tormented forever and ever. The righteous in this group will be saved. Why should you assign yourself to that terrible place of divine retribution? Jesus took our wrath for us when he went to Calvary and shed his own blood. He took our sins upon himself. He endured the wrath of a holy God. He died and rose again for our justification.

Whosoever's name is not found written in the book of life will be cast into the lake of fire. God is the keeper of the book of life. Is your name written in there? You need to ask Jesus to forgive you of your sins. You need to ask him to cleanse you with his precious blood. You must ask him to save you and give you eternal life. You must turn your back to sin and give him your whole heart. He will abundantly forgive you and save you. You must invite his Holy Spirit into your life.

REVELATION CHAPTER 21

Revelation 21:1–3 states, "And I saw a new heaven and a new earth: for the first heaven and the first earth were passed away; and there was no more sea. And I John saw the holy city, New Jerusalem, coming down from God out of heaven, prepared as a bride adorned for her husband. And I heard a great voice out of heaven saying, Behold, the tabernacle of God is with men, and he will dwell with them, and they shall be his people, and God himself shall be with them, and be their God."

Second Peter 3:10–14 reads as follows:

> But the day of the Lord will come as a thief in the night; in the which the heavens shall pass away with a great noise, and the elements shall melt with fervent heat, the earth also and the works that are therein shall be burned up. Seeing then that all these things shall be dissolved, what manner of persons ought ye to be in all holy conversation and godliness,

looking for and hasting unto the coming of the day of God, wherein the heavens being on fire shall be dissolved, and the elements shall melt with fervent heat? Nevertheless we, according to his promise, look for new heavens and a new earth, wherein dwelleth righteousness. Wherefore, beloved, seeing that ye look for such things, be diligent that ye may be found of him in peace, without spot, and blameless.

Isaiah 66:22 states, "For as the new heavens and the new earth, which I will make, shall remain before me, saith the Lord, so shall your seed and your name remain."

The redeemed of the Lord shall inherit the paradise that God has prepared for them.

This great city reveals God's great architectural skill and designs. There is no city built by humankind that even comes close to being comparable to the city of God. This city is the home of his bride, the wife of Christ. We are going to enjoy God forever and ever and bask in the glory of his presence. God himself shall be there. The emphatic pronoun *himself* is used, so we know beyond a shadow of a doubt that he will dwell among his people, not metaphorically but literally. We shall see his face and be able to withstand his awesome presence. We will be equipped with glorified bodies just like Jesus. We are flesh of his flesh, and bone of his bones (Ephesians 5:30).

We will worship God through the countless ages of eternity. The greatest honor God can give to any living creature of his creation is the ability to come into his presence and bow before His Excellent Majesty!

Revelation 21:4 reads, "And God shall wipe away all tears from their eyes; and there shall be no more death, neither sorrow, nor crying, neither shall there be any more pain: for the former things are passed away." Glory to God!

God's new paradise will be an eternity of love, joy, and peace.

It will be an eternity of banqueting. Remember the parable of the prodigal son when he returned home to his father? Luke 15:20–25 tells the story:

> And he arose, and came to his father. But when he was yet a great way off, his father saw him, and had compassion, and ran, and fell on his neck, and kissed him. And the son said unto him, Father, I have sinned against heaven, and in thy sight, and am no worthier to be called thy son. But the father said to his servants, bring forth the best robe, and put it on him; and put a ring on his hand, and shoes on his feet: and bring hither the fatted calf, and kill it; and let us eat, and be merry: For this my son was dead, and is alive again; he was lost, and is found. And they began to be merry. Now his elder son was in the field: and as he came and drew nigh to the house, he heard music and dancing.

Are you trading the pleasures of this world for the pleasures that God has provided for those who love him? I encourage you to forsake your sins and, like the prodigal son, come back to God. Call upon the name of the Lord and you shall be saved.

Revelation 21:5 reads, "And he that sat upon the throne said, Behold, I make all things new. And he said unto me, Write: for these words are true and faithful."

First Corinthians 2:9–10 states, "But as it is written, Eye hath not seen, nor ear heard, neither have entered into the heart of man, the things which God hath prepared for them that love him. But God hath revealed them unto us by his Spirit: for the Spirit searcheth all things, yea, the deep things of God."

We read in Revelation 21:6–7, "And he said unto me, It is done. I am Alpha and Omega, the beginning and the end. I will give unto him that is athirst of the fountain of the water of life freely. He that overcometh shall inherit all things; and I will be his God, and he shall be my son."

The New Testament was originally written in Greek. The first letter in the Greek alphabet is *alpha*, and the last letter is *omega*. So here God is relating to us that he is the beginning and the ending of all things. He knows the end from the beginning, and therefore we can rely on everything he reveals and says. He is the author and finisher of our faith!

First John 3:1–3 states, "Behold, what manner of love the Father hath bestowed upon us, that we should be called the sons of God: therefore the world knoweth us not, because it knew him not. Beloved, now are we the sons of God, and it doth not yet appear what we shall be: but we know that, when he shall appear, we shall be like him; for we shall see him as he is. And every man that hath this hope in him purifieth himself, even as he is pure."

Romans 8:16–19 states, "The Spirit itself beareth witness with our spirit, that we are the children of God: And if children, then heirs; heirs of God, and joint-heirs with Christ; if so be that we suffer with him, that we may be also glorified together. For I reckon that the sufferings of this present time are not worthy to be compared with the glory which shall be revealed in us. For the earnest expectation of the creature waiteth for the manifestation of the sons of God."

We read in Revelation 21:8, "But the fearful, and unbelieving, and the abominable, and murderers, and sexually immoral, and sorcerers, and idolaters, and all liars, shall have their part in the lake which burneth with fire and brimstone: which is the second death."

You have one choice to make in this matter: (1) Choose God and his righteousness and be saved. (2) Reject God and choose this world's sinful pleasures and be lost forever.

First John 2:15–17 states, "Love not the world, neither the things that are in the world. If any man love the world, the love of the Father is not in him. For all that is in the world, the lust of the flesh, and the lust of the eyes, and the pride of life, is not of the Father, but is of the world. And the world passeth away, and the lust thereof: but he that doeth the will of God abideth forever."

We read in Revelation 21:9–11, "And there came unto me one of the seven angels which had the seven vials full of the seven last plagues, and talked with me, saying, Come hither, I will show thee the bride, the Lamb's wife. And he carried me away in the spirit to a great and high mountain, and showed me that great city, the holy Jerusalem, descending out of heaven from God, having the glory of God: and her light was like unto a stone most precious, even like a jasper stone, clear as crystal."

The time has come for the true church of Jesus Christ to inherit the glorious mansions that God has provided for each and every one of us. The honeymoon is over as the thousand-year reign with Christ and his saints has come to an end on this old earth. The glorious city is now occupied by the Lamb's wife. What a splendor. The church bears the glory of God. Now the city that she lives in also bears the glory of God. God himself shall be there. Triple glory!

Revelation 21:12–14 states, "And had a wall great and high, and had twelve gates, and at the gates twelve angels, and names written thereon, which are the names of the twelve tribes of the children of Israel: On the east three gates; on the north three gates; on the south three gates; and on the west three gates. And the wall of the city had twelve foundations, and in them the names of the twelve apostles of the Lamb."

The angels who guard the city carry the same names of the twelve sons of Jacob/Israel.

The church is built upon the doctrines of the apostles of the Lamb of God and upon Jesus, the chief cornerstone.

Revelation 21:15–16 reads, "And he that talked with me had a golden reed to measure the city, and the gates thereof, and the wall thereof. And the city lieth foursquare, and the length is as large as the breadth: and he measured the city with the reed, twelve thousand furlongs. The length and the breadth and the height of it are equal."

Twelve thousand furlongs equals fifteen hundred miles, so the city, New Jerusalem, which will be the capital of the new earth, will be fifteen hundred miles long by fifteen hundred miles wide by fifteen hundred miles high, filled with mansions of varying heights rising high into the sky. Wow! There will be enough mansions there in that glorious city for every child of God to have one. The building will be in the form of a glorious cube.

Revelation 21:17 reads, "And he measured the wall thereof, an hundred and forty and four cubits, according to the measure of a man, that is, of the angel." God gives in detail the literal, actual measurements.

We read the following in Revelation 21:18–21:

> And the building of the wall of it was of jasper: and the city was pure gold, like unto clear glass. And the foundations of the wall of the city were garnished with all manner of precious stones. The first foundation was jasper; the second, sapphire; the third, a chalcedony; the fourth, an emerald; The fifth, sardonyx; the sixth, sardius; the seventh, chrysolite; the eighth, beryl; the ninth, a topaz; the tenth, a chrysoprasus; the eleventh, a jacinth; the twelfth, an amethyst. And the twelve gates were twelve pearls; every several gate was of one pearl: and the street of the city was pure gold, as it were transparent glass.

The structure of this city, the home of the redeemed, will be made not of bricks and ordinary stones but of jasper, the most precious stone in the universe. The gold of the city will be so refined by divine means and ability that it will look like glass. Wow! O the love of God toward us is so great that we cannot fathom it.

Revelation 21:22–23 reads, "And I saw no temple therein: for the Lord God Almighty and the Lamb are the temple of it. And the city had no need of the sun, neither of the moon, to shine in it: for the glory of God did lighten it, and the *Lamb is the light thereof*" (emphasis added). Although there are designated areas for worship, for example, the area marked before the throne and the sea of glass, notice that the Lamb of God bears the glory that lightens the city. The glory of God did lighten it but the Lamb is its light! The light is coming from the Lamb. The glory of God is the glory of the Lamb. They are inseparable. In John 17:5, Jesus prays, "And now, O Father, glorify thou me with thine own self with the glory which I had with thee before the world was."

You will notice in Revelation chapter 22 that the throne that God sits upon is the same throne that the Lamb sits upon. The Jehovah of the Old Testament is the Jesus of the New Testament. He only became flesh for the work of redemption.

First Timothy 3:16 states, "And without controversy great is the mystery of godliness: God was manifest in the flesh, justified in the Spirit, seen of angels, preached unto the Gentiles, believed on in the world, received up into glory."

We read in Revelation 21:24–25, "And the nations of them which are saved shall walk in the light of it: and the kings of the earth do bring their glory and honor into it. And the gates of it shall not be shut at all by day: for there shall be no night there."

Apart from the church, there are other categories of saints. There are the people who will be saved during the thousand-year reign of Christ (Psalm 72:8–14).

You cannot be a part of these glorious promises unless you come to Jesus and allow his precious blood to wash you and cleanse you from sin.

First John 1:7–9 states, "But if we walk in the light, as he is in the light, we have fellowship one with another, and the blood of Jesus Christ his Son cleanseth us from all sin. If we say that we have no sin, we deceive ourselves, and the truth is not in us. If we confess our sins, he is faithful and just to forgive us our sins, and to cleanse us from all unrighteousness."

Revelation 21:25 reads, "And the gates of it shall not be shut at all by day: for there shall be no night there." This describes God's plan of eternal rest for his children. After all our labors for him, we shall rest in his eternal delights, a period of time when there will be no more night.

Hebrews 4:8–11 states, "For if Jesus had given them rest, then would he not afterward have spoken of another day. There remaineth therefore a rest to the people of God. For he that is entered into his rest, he also hath ceased from his own works, as God did from his. Let us labour therefore to enter into that rest, lest any man fall after the same example of unbelief."

We read in Revelation 21:26–27, "And they shall bring the glory and honor of the nations into it. And there shall in no wise enter into it anything that defileth, neither whatsoever worketh abomination, nor maketh a lie: but they which are written in the Lamb's book of life."

The wife of Christ (the church) will be treated as special royalty. The nations that are saved will be delighted to bring the best of their continued produce to be consumed by the inhabitants of the city of New Jerusalem.

Is your name written in the book of life? You may have your name written in a religious book, but more important than that, is your name written in the Lamb's book of life? For unless it is, you cannot enter heaven. You will not be a part of the bride.

Please say the following prayer from your heart:

> Dear Lord, Maker of heaven and earth, I come to you in the precious name of Jesus Christ. Your Word teaches me that I am a sinner and need a Savior. I believe that Jesus Christ is the Son of God who died for my sins. I believe that he lived a life without sin and rose from the dead. I believe his blood that he shed on Calvary was for me. I believe Jesus ascended to heaven and is seated at the right hand of God, and that he is coming back for me. Please, dear Lord, forgive me of all my sins. Come into my heart today. Come in to stay. I give up my sins, and by your grace I will live the rest of my life for your praise and glory.

Thank you, Lord Jesus, for hearing my prayer and for saving me in Jesus's name. Amen.

REVELATION CHAPTER 22

Revelation 22:1 reads, "And he showed me a pure river of water of life, clear as crystal, proceeding out of the throne of God and of the Lamb."

Indeed, God is so gracious that he provides for his children a river of water of life. It flows from the throne. God is the Author of life. Without him there is no life. When Moses struck the rock in the wilderness, water came out of it. The striking of the rock symbolizes Calvary and the work of grace that was fulfilled when Jesus gave his life so that we may live through his life. First Corinthians 10:1–4 states, "Moreover, brethren, I would not that ye should be ignorant, how that all our fathers were under the cloud, and all passed through the sea; and were all baptized unto Moses in the cloud and in the sea; and did all eat the same spiritual meat; and did all drink the same spiritual drink: for they drank of that spiritual Rock that followed them: and that Rock was Christ." The actuality of the Lamb's sacrifice and the river that flows from the throne of God, clear as crystal, is an eternal truth reminding us of the goodness of God in providing eternal redemption for humankind. Note that there is only one throne upon which God and the Lamb (Jesus) sit. Jesus told his disciples, "In that day ye shall know that I am in the Father and the Father in me."

Revelation 22:2 reads, "In the midst of the street of it, and on either side of the river, was there the tree of life, which bare twelve manner of fruits, and yielded her fruit every month: and the leaves of the tree were for the healing of the nations."

The tree of life, which was taken away from Adam and Eve in the Garden of Eden, is now permanently placed in the midst of the river of life that flows from the throne of God and the Lamb. What a blessing! It's a double blessing to be able to eat from the tree of life and drink from the river of life. The privilege to drink and eat will not be to satisfy hunger and thirst but will be as a delightful pleasure, because in that city we shall neither hunger nor thirst again.

The tree of life is like a deep-rooted vine tree stretching itself along the river of life on both sides. The distance it stretches along the river is not known. It bears twelve different types of fruits every month. God is a God of variety. There will be no monotony in heaven. It will be a tree always bearing fruits for the redeemed. There will be no scarcity or lack of delightful pleasures in this new heaven or on this new earth that God promises us. The leaves of the tree will be for the healing of the nations. The nations that are round about and beyond the city will need the leaves from the tree of life to maintain their eternal vibrancy.

Revelation 22:3–4 reads, "And there shall be no more curse: but the throne of God and of the Lamb shall be in it; and his servants shall serve him: And they shall see his face; and his name shall be in their foreheads."

Note that *throne* is used and not *thrones*. The Lamb sits upon the throne of God in the final analysis. There shall be no more curse. God did curse the ground for humankind's sake and brought judgment upon the woman in terms of her bringing forth children with birth pains (Genesis chapter 3). But there shall be no curse in the new heaven or on the new earth. Jesus took our curse when he went to the cross. Galatians 3:13–14 states, "Christ hath redeemed us from the curse of the law, being made a curse for us: for it is written, Cursed is every one that hangeth on a tree: that the blessing of Abraham might come on the Gentiles through Jesus Christ; that we might receive the promise of the Spirit through faith."

Now we serve him by faith, but in the new heaven and on the new earth we shall see the face of God.

First Corinthians 13:12 states, "For now we see through a glass, darkly; but then face to face: now I know in part; but then shall I know even as also I am known."

Second Corinthians 3:18 states, "But we all, with open face beholding as in a glass the glory of the Lord, are changed into the same image from glory to glory, even as by the Spirit of the Lord."

We read in Revelation 22:5, "And there shall be no night there;

and they need no candle, neither light of the sun; for the Lord God giveth them light: and they shall reign for ever and ever."

Again, Matthew 13:43 states, "Then shall the righteous *shine forth as the sun* in the kingdom of their Father. Who hath ears to hear, let him hear" (emphasis added).

Daniel 12:2–3 states, "And many of them that sleep in the dust of the earth shall awake, some to everlasting life, and some to shame and everlasting contempt. And they that be wise shall shine as the brightness of the firmament; and they that turn many to righteousness as the stars for ever and ever."

We read in Revelation 22:6, "And he said unto me, These sayings are faithful and true: and the Lord God of the holy prophets sent his angel to shew unto his servants the things which must shortly be done."

God gives us the assurance that the revelation shall come to pass, and he stands to ensure that it remains true and faithful. God backs up his promises. It shall come to pass even as he has revealed.

Revelation 22:7 reads, "Behold, I come quickly: blessed is he that keepeth the sayings of the prophecy of this book." The hour of his coming is much closer than it was when the church was born on the Day of Pentecost.

Revelation 22:8–9 reads, "And I John saw these things, and heard them. And when I had heard and seen, I fell down to worship before the feet of the angel which shewed me these things. Then saith he unto me, See thou do it not: for I am thy fellowservant, and of thy brethren the prophets, and of them which keep the sayings of this book: worship God."

John's heart was so full of gratitude that he fell down to worship the angel, but the angel directed him to worship God. When we read the book of Revelation, our hearts, like John's, should be filled with such gratitude that worshipping God should be our spontaneous reaction.

Revelation 22:10 reads, "And he saith unto me, Seal not the sayings of the prophecy of this book: for the time is at hand."

It's interesting to know that about 600 BC, when Daniel got the revelation from God concerning the end times, the angel said to him, "Go thy way, Daniel: for the words are closed up and sealed till the time of the end" (Daniel 12:9).

In this verse, the angel tells John, "Seal not the sayings of the prophecy of this book: for the time is at hand." Get ready: Jesus is coming soon!

Revelation 22:13 states, "I am Alpha and Omega, the beginning and the end, the first and the last."

In Revelation 1:11, when John heard a voice as if hearing a trumpet behind him, saying, "I am Alpha and Omega, the first and the last," he looked behind him and saw that it was the Son of man, Jesus, speaking to him. You cannot get away from this doctrine. Jesus is God, the only God. Note that the book of Revelation is the revelation of Jesus by God.

We read in Revelation 22:14–15, "Blessed are they that do his commandments that they may have right to the tree of life, and may enter in through the gates into the city. For without are dogs, and sorcerers, and sexually immoral, and murderers, and idolaters, and whosoever loveth and maketh a lie."

The commandments here are not the Ten Commandments, but the teachings of the gospel of grace.

Second Corinthians 3:6–8 states, "Who also hath made us able ministers of the New Testament; not of the letter, but of the spirit: for the letter killeth, but the spirit giveth life. But if the ministration of death, written and engraven in stones, was glorious, so that the children of Israel could not steadfastly behold the face of Moses for the glory of his countenance; which glory was to be done away: How shall not the ministration of the spirit be rather glorious?"

Revelation 22:16 reads, "I Jesus have sent mine angel to testify unto you these things in the churches. I am the root and the offspring of David, and the bright and morning star."

Salvation is of the Jews. Acts 4:12 says, "Neither is there salvation in any other: for there is none other name under heaven given among men, whereby we must be saved."

We read in Revelation 22:17, "And the Spirit and the bride say,

Come. And let him that heareth say, Come. And let him that is athirst come. And whosoever will, let him take the water of life freely." What a great invitation. It is for whosever will accept!

> In Matthew 11:28–30, Jesus says, "Come unto me, all ye that labour and are heavy laden, and I will give you rest. Take my yoke upon you, and learn of me; for I am meek and lowly in heart: and ye shall find rest unto your souls. For my yoke is easy, and my burden is light."

We read in Revelation 22:18–19, "For I testify unto every man that heareth the words of the prophecy of this book, If any man shall add unto these things, God shall add unto him the plagues that are written in this book: And if any man shall take away from the words of the book of this prophecy, God shall take away his part out of the book of life, and out of the holy city, and from the things which are written in this book."

The Lord Jesus forewarns us not to add anything to or take away anything from this book. It's so accurate and true that to tamper with it would be met with swift judgment of damnation. In Matthew 24:35, Jesus says, "Heaven and earth shall pass away, but my words shall not pass away."

Revelation 22:20–21 reads, "He which testifieth these things saith, Surely I come quickly. Amen. Even so, come, Lord Jesus. The grace of our Lord Jesus Christ be with you all. Amen."

Jesus is coming back for his bride at the rapture. He is coming back with his wife at the battle of Armageddon to reign for a thousand years, and then he will set up his eternal kingdom in the new heaven and on the new earth. Even so, come, Lord Jesus, come!

The grace, love, and mercy of our Lord Jesus is what will make us worthy partakers of all these precious promises of God. Amen.

PART THREE

The Prophetic
Page

CHAPTER FOUR

The Prophecy

ᘓ◞ ──────────────────────────

Hello again, reader. I hope and pray that today will be a good day for your soul. God is not willing that any should perish but that all will come to repentance. This scripture is found in 2 Peter 3:9. Now let's read Isaiah 21:11–12: "The burden of Dumah. He calleth to me out of Seir, Watchman, what of the night? Watchman, what of the night? The watchman said, *The morning cometh, and also the night*: if ye will enquire, enquire ye: *return, come*" (emphasis added).

In Daniel 12:2–3 we read, "And many of them that sleep in the dust of the earth shall awake, some to everlasting life, and some to shame and everlasting contempt. And they that be wise shall shine as the brightness of the firmament; and they that turn many to righteousness as the stars for ever and ever."

John 5:28–29 states, "Marvel not at this: for the hour is coming, in the which all that are in the graves shall hear his voice, and shall come forth; they that have done good, unto the resurrection of life; and they that have done evil, unto the resurrection of damnation."

Yes, the watchman says, the morning cometh, so also cometh the night. It will be morning for all those who accept Jesus as their personal Savior, but it will be night for those who reject him. God gave the faithful watchman a prophetic eagle eye to see into the future. He was amazed to see two opposites occurring one after the next. He saw the morning cometh; certainly this speaks of the glorious day when the saints will be resurrected, given glorified bodies, and made partakers of God's eternal kingdom. But coming also is the night. The night is coming certainly for the unrepentant, the sinner who dies in his sins. He also will be resurrected but to shame and everlasting contempt. Will you have a morning of eternal bliss, or will you have a night of eternal torture and torment? The watchman saw what will happen to our souls. The choice is ours; the decision is yours. The result belongs to God. The morning cometh, and so too does the night.

The watchman says, "Come. Will you *come* to Jesus and be saved?" Jesus says in John 6:37, "All that the Father giveth me shall come to me; and him that cometh to me I will in no wise cast out." Isaiah 1:18 reads, "*Come* now, and let us reason together, saith the Lord: though your sins be as scarlet, they shall be as white as snow; though they be red like crimson, they shall be as wool" (emphasis added).

Matthew 11:28–30 says, "Come unto me, all ye that labour and are heavy laden, and I will give you rest. Take my yoke upon you, and learn of me; for I am meek and lowly in heart: and ye shall find rest unto your souls. For my yoke is easy, and my burden is light."

The watchman also says, "Return." Will you return? Isaiah 55:7 says, "Let the wicked forsake his way, and the unrighteous man his thoughts: and let him *return* unto the Lord, and he will have mercy upon him; and to our God, for he will abundantly pardon" (emphasis added).

Now let's get down to the business of this chapter. Amos 3:7 states, "Surely the Lord God will do nothing, but he revealeth his secret unto his servants the prophets." I wish here to operate in the revelation Jesus gave to his disciples in John 16:13, which states, "Howbeit when he, the Spirit of truth, is come, he will guide you into all truth: for he shall not speak of himself; but whatsoever he shall hear, that shall he speak: *and he will shew you things to come*" (emphasis added).

Prophecy can be looked at in two ways: (1) as telling forth and (2) as foretelling. Revelation 19:10 reads, "And I fell at his feet to worship him. And he said unto me, See thou do it not: I am thy fellow servants, and of thy brethren that have the testimony of Jesus: worship God: for the testimony of Jesus is the spirit of prophecy." If, for example, I should proclaim that Jesus is coming again, that is telling forth, that is, saying what the written Word has already said. But the following example is one of foretelling of an event before it is written. Acts 11:28 reads, "And there stood up one of them named Agabus, and signified by the Spirit that there should be great dearth throughout all the world: which came to pass in the days of Claudius Caesar."

I would like to make a few prophetic utterances in the area of foretelling.

- When will the one world government begin? Answer: between 2025 and 2026.
- How old will the Antichrist be when he takes office? Answer: sixty-three years. When he is sixty-one years of age, he will hold a leading position in world politics or influence. When he takes up office, the back of his head will be partly bald.

Now let's do some telling forth about him. He will be of mixed origin, half White and half Black. Revelation 13:2 says, "He looks like a leopard." A leopard has black and white spots.

His feet are described as the feet of a bear. This speaks of his political strength. His mouth is as the mouth of a lion. This speaks of his military might. He will emerge from a powerful military country. He will come from the west (Daniel 11:36–45). In the latter end of his reign, the kings of the north, the south, and the east will come against him. Where is he located? It must be understood that he will not come against himself, so he is located in the *west*.

When will the battle of Armageddon occur? In the seventh year of the reign of the Antichrist. Time is short; Jesus is coming soon. Let's be ready! Again I say that Jesus is coming soon!

If these prophetic statements are of me, they will fail to materialize, but if they are of the Lord, they shall come to pass just as I have written in *The Life-Giving Tree.*

Printed in the United States
by Baker & Taylor Publisher Services